PINCH ME

FRANCESCA RAMSAY is an art historian and writer based in Bristol. *Pinch Me* is her first book.

PINCH ME

TRYING TO FEEL REAL IN THE 21st CENTURY

FRANCESCA RAMSAY

First published in Great Britain in 2023 by Ortac Press

ISBN: 978-1-8383887-7-5

A CIP record for this book is available from the British Library

Cover artwork by Grace Attlee
Cover design by Anna Morrison

Set in LD Fabiol by Tetragon, London
Printed and bound by CPI Group (UK) Ltd, Croydon, CRO 4YY

ortacpress.com

For my parents.
Without doubt.

I could be
Here and now
I would be, I should be
But how?

NICK DRAKE
One of These Things First

I AM SWIMMING. It is very late, or perhaps early in the morning. Time is irrelevant. Out and out I swim into the softened landscape, with the dark sky the same temperature as the water and the water the same temperature as me. I might be flying, for all I can tell. All is velvet and all is alone, the ocean beneath me mirroring the impossible depth of the night sky. And all I know in this moment is that this moment is *now*. With such an astounding and rare certainty I am – for just one instant – present, real and right here.

The water delineates and expounds me.

PINCH ME.

I'm a will-o'-the-wisp, all shadow and ether.

For as long as I can remember I have lived at a distance from my own life, hovering a few millimetres behind my eyes and just above my hairline. That's not to say I don't enjoy living. Like the rest of us, I cry with laughter and frustration, I fall in and out of love. I bruise easily. I am badly dressed. But the varying levels of disconnect I have to the rest of the world leave me convinced I must be sleepwalking. I'm split in two, mind and body rarely able to be in the same place at the same time; in the now and now and now of moment-by-moment existence. Reality should be as simple as breathing, but it's not. Perhaps you feel it too? Perhaps you share this same sense of dislocation from your own life? Perhaps, like me, you believe there must be more.

There have been moments, see; pinpricks in time that have given me such an essential and triumphant feeling of realness I am for that one split second jolted directly back into myself. I have found it when immersed in bodies of very cold water, when face-to-face with a vast and beautiful view. I have found it in print, loud noise and in utter silence. I have found it in darkness too. But most of all, most consistently, I have found it in art. There have been paintings that have grabbed me by both shoulders and stopped me still in their presence; drawings so intricate, so concentrate, that they demand my full awareness, whispering to me this question:

'Could you be anywhere else but here, now, in this exact moment?'

For the rest of the time though – like a forgotten word on the tongue, or the deeply recognisable landscape of a dream lost just after waking – I have nothing but a dusty feeling that, if I tried just a little harder, I would be on the cusp of something truly magnificent.

I refuse to exist like this any longer. This is my journey to find reality in the twenty-first century.

But before we begin, I'd like to clarify a few things.

Firstly, it feels important to bring up just how *many* options there are to ground, connect and bring ourselves into the present today. It sure has captured the zeitgeist, reality; we're all after it, and there seem to be innumerable methods with which to form a closer relationship both to it and to ourselves. And so I would like to admit before we really get started that this is a far from comprehensive study. It is instead a personal exploration: sparking, I hope, what might become a similar journey of your own.

I would also like to make it clear that this is not a book about mental health. I am by no means an expert on this, and would certainly feel uncomfortable touting myself as one. On saying that though, it would have been perverse of me to ignore the links between my disconnection from reality, with anxiety and depression. Each feeds into the next. And this is true for us all.

Contemporary life *can* cause us to feel increasingly anxious and/or depressed. Our brain *can* react to this uncomfortable present by turning on the dissociation switch and disconnecting us from the here and now. I can't write about one without writing about the others.

But most importantly, before we get going at all, I'd like to talk about men. Male artists, in particular. Over the course of writing this book, the following uncomfortable truth dawned on me: that the majority of the works that have struck such a chord in my heart, the paintings that get right to the crux of the issue I'm exploring here, have been made by men. And even worse, that the painting that really set off this whole journey wasn't made by just any man but was by Picasso. I mean, he was hardly a harbinger of women's rights.

Art history is such a historically male space it is even entrenched in the language which we use to discuss it. And that's not just *masterpiece*, *masterful* and *old master*, but the word *genius*, too. A problematic word that's inherently linked to white male privilege, genius welcomes misogyny with open arms, transforming female artists into lovers and wives rather than success stories in their own right. And as Linda Nochlin argued in 1971 in her seminal essay 'Why Have There Been No Great Women Artists?', it couldn't have gone any other way – *of course* those who've been offered education, power, the right to vote and to control their own finances and bodies will have excelled, when compared to those who had none of these options.

The artworks I've chosen to write about are a reflection of my *exposure* to art; a mirror in particular to a visual education that began way before any academic one. And a mirror to an education and access that continues to sit within a patriarchal society. But not to write about the artists that have struck me in this strange and particular way would have been to lie. Because in essence, these are the artists that have shown me what it is to feel real. And in doing so, they have given me the freedom to feel it myself.

Picasso was many things, but overarchingly, he was *free*. His art is joyful, it's creative and playful, and it's no wonder. With the ability to exist exactly as he wished – to eat, drink and feel as he wanted, to socialise and sleep with anyone who caught his eye – each of his works (even when dealing with the most difficult of subject matters) is an embodiment of a life lived with total freedom. And I think, at the crux of it, this is what has drawn me to these works. They exist as spaces within which anyone can hold the huge and powerful feelings that life often doesn't allow. Created by people with the freedom to feel, they can be nothing but.

My love for these works feels as much an affectation as anything else. It is a love that sits uncomfortable and awkward inside of me – has little in common (I'd like to think) with the rest of it. And so I'd like to clarify that this is not a recommended list. I'd love for you to make your own, and I will be using this as a lesson to build on mine.

And finally, because *Pinch Me* is a book about *feeling* real, it would be a mistake, before I properly begin, not to question what this feeling is in the first place, and to ask especially what it might look like today. Life, it seems, has become ever fictionalised. Some moments, it's true, are so big that they *should* be fiction, unable to fit onto the small screen of our own lives. Like sobbing drunk on a London night bus; eighty percent heartbroken, the other twenty feeling absolutely iconic. Technology has made our distance from the real far worse, though this is partly our own fault. We curate our own fictions. Free to pick and choose our own realities, we use our smartphones to enlighten us at the same time as draw us away. And draw us away from other people too. Because it's a lonely thing, existing in this multitude of divisions. Technology has not just brought about a divorce from each other but a divorce from the physical, allowing existence in two dimensions simultaneously.[1] (We straddle two realities, occupying neither enough to weigh in on much at all.)

When I began seriously thinking about the ideas behind this book, I soon realised two things. The first was that I've actually been searching for reality most of my life, in one way or another. So in part, these coming pages will be a memento to the unconscious explorations I've already made. *Pinch Me* will document a vicarious journey through, first and foremost, art and its creators, but also noise, space and through silence. This is a book drenched in water, a book that spans whole landscapes and the expanse of the skies. Within these pages there will be body and ego and self. And I hope, *I hope,* there will be spirit. Down one of these many and varied paths, I am determined to find reality. I seek existence in no uncertain terms.

The second realisation I have is that I'm not alone. Again and again I have conversations with friends where we all agree on this same niggling feeling. That we're waiting for our proper lives to begin; that all of this is just fooling about, we're wasting our time – all of us struggling with a sense of removal from the way things are panning out for us. I sometimes have the feeling that I exist somewhere on the edge of my life, rather than being directly inside it. This might be that I am still right at the beginning, and though I am all grown, nobody told me how to really get started. So I'm just hanging around, doing this and that, waiting to set my real life in motion. Or it could be the opposite: that I've got all the way to the end without realising. And so this is me looking back on a life, a half-remembered film reel of a person I don't quite recognise. What has got us to this point today? Why have we dissociated from the present moment? Distraction, globalisation, technology, poor mental health: these are only a scattering of today's issues that will be spun into my journey. But this book will be neither dry nor analytic. It's a call to arms. A call to live life until it's tattered and dog-eared. A call to live life with a deep and resounding sense of reality. We'd do well to heed the words of the nineteenth-century naturalist Henry David Thoreau when he tells us, 'Above all, we cannot afford not to live in the present'.[2]

But what is this reality I am looking for? It is a rare and beautiful thing. I am done with the hazy and half-replica. Reality for me is truth. It is hyper-awareness and presence and clarity, it is *being* rather than not quite bothering to wake up. Reality is both loud and peaceful, is minuscule yet mighty, is outside of me, is all of me, completes and disappears me (reality for me can be quite the contradiction). I want it under my fingernails and in my pores. I want it like glue to bind my mind to my body and my body to the earth. I want it to snub those cruel Cartesian rationalists who cleaved mind from body over three hundred years ago (and when I find it I will sew myself back together and parade in front of this philosophy that states the two are separate things). I want reality rich and peaty and the colour of bracken. I want each one of its seven letters. I want it in all its vastness I want it blue. Reality ties together the whole of time. Sometimes I think that it can be nothing more than a stitch or two.

For me, reality should be as simple as coming home. I dream of it often, home; a landscape made up of steep and weathered hills (each dream a different season). I dream of cliff tops that invite me to walk for miles along them, my only companion the wild ocean far below. I dream of tumbled houses, an old windmill and winding streets. The sense of home, and more than that, the sense of reality in these dreams, is so hugging and certain I feel as if I have known these places all my life. That I have never left, nor needed to. It's a heartbreaking contradiction of an awakening, to open one's eyes and immediately slide from dream reality into dream-like existence. In these most disjointed moments I go to sleep wondering if I will wake up having aged forty years. Time seems irretrievably flaky. Of course the next morning, all blurred edges and unshakeable sleep, I'm only a few hours older. But I can never quite trust it.

This sense of home feels profoundly important in my search for reality. But I don't think I am looking for it in its traditional concept. Rather than the home that a house can provide, it is something closer to the connectedness to place one has as a child; those roots that bind you to your small known world. It is the spiritual and physical assuredness that is so beautifully coupled with a child's naivety. The age before nostalgia, before missing. It makes sense to me that home should be our centre of gravity. And if it is true that it is at the beating heart of all our emotions, then reality must lie close.

Reality is hard to picture if you've always had it. But perhaps you can imagine this. You're walking from platform to platform of a huge underground station. It's rush hour. You're trying to block out the sound of some busker playing the didgeridoo. There are people everywhere and you're exhausted. You're breathing the same recycled air and pushing against the crowds; being more physically intimate with strangers than you have been with anyone all day. But at the same time, you're completely separate. Like everyone else, you're just looking into the middle distance. And because you're bored of doing the same thing day in, day out – and like I said, you're tired and maybe a little on edge – you zone out slightly. If I were to pinch you, perhaps you wouldn't feel it at all. Reality takes second place; you distance yourself from the present. Just trying to get home.

Just trying to get home.

In a picture, it should be possible to discover new things every time you see it. But you can look at a picture for a week and never think of it again. You can also look at a picture for a second and think of it all of your life.

JOAN MIRÓ

I

Painting

THIS IS WHAT DID IT. A heavy ceramic white jug, four golden-brown and rough-textured russets, a wooden table. Nothing more than that.

No. Everything more than that.

We look at each other, the painting and I, and all else in the room is irrelevant. It stops me stock-still, giving me a *bada-boom bada-boom* in my chest like some lust-struck cartoon character. All I am is heart and eyes and body washed cool right through with tones of blue and green and grey. All I am is wrapped up in its generous curves; the jug painted with as much intimacy as a long-familiar lover; the outright eroticism of its lip; the smooth swoop of its belly the sexualised centre of a sixteenth-century Italian nude. It is Titian's *Venus d'Urbino* in kitchen china.

And this is how it happens. Just for that one small shiver, one beautiful moment of a pure and unexpected clarity. A sudden arrival of being. I feel real.

I leave the museum clutching a postcard. It's a mockery, really, of what I have just experienced, but still it will serve as a reminder that, somewhere, this sense of reality truly does exist inside of me. I can feel the painting's presence all the way down the stairs – a lovely buoyed coolness, as if I am walking down a small waterfall. And then out I go into the sun-brittled Parisian morning. The clarity I felt in the museum is swept away with the streams of tourists. Reality slipping out of my fingers with the same sudden ease as it had arrived.

Something inside me sparks, fizzes. Faults. (The crack and nothing of a blown bulb.)

I am in Paris chaperoning a group of rich American teenagers. I don't speak French, have been to Paris once before for the sum-total of fourteen hours (of which I spent much lost in the depths of the metro system), and am unequivocally bad at pastoral care. I blindly lead my little flock up the Eiffel Tower, to Notre-Dame, shopping on the Champs-Élysées. I forget to save their mobile numbers and lose nearly all of them in the Louvre. When I take them on a Ferris wheel I become so irrationally and immediately scared of heights I lose the power of speech entirely. It is hardly the Grand Tour.

A lot of my time is spent supervising their incessant mood swings; I barely manage to mask my own. When one has a tantrum on the metro I lean in close and whisper, 'I know you're faking it' and then ignore him for the rest of the journey. It is a surprise to the both of us when this method works. There's another one, Tyler, who is the son of a multi-millionaire West Coast Republican. He has a maid, and a kitchen in his family home that has never been used. Tyler says things like 'My dad takes me on NRA marches' – and, when I ask him about his future plans, 'politics'. He is, unfortunately, completely adorable. Tyler buys so many ludicrously expensive plastic souvenirs (including a three-foot replica of the Eiffel Tower) he has to get them crated up and shipped back to LA.

Right at the end of the trip, I take them all out for dinner at a sushi restaurant. We spend the remainder of the evening at the fairground, where I watch their blurred and screaming faces whip past me. One is so magnificently sick she has to be publicly hosed down by two fair attendants. She veers between laughter and tears; adolescence as the quintessential tragi-comedy.

Every day half of me stays asleep under the fan in my hotel bedroom, and the other half gets on with the job, buzzed up on too many tiny coffees and floating somewhere just beyond my head. It is only the paintings that seem to wake me up from this walking dream: my experience in the Musée Picasso the most startling of shocks into full consciousness.

See, they catch me off guard, paintings. It is as if they were magnetic; or the promise of water on a hot day, quenching and immediate. I have stood in front of artworks all over the place filled up with something bigger than myself – an abstract bubble of adrenaline or emotion, I don't quite know what. When it happens, I have to leave immediately whichever gallery or museum I am in, averting my eyes from any other wall, I'm that terrified of deflating the feeling. Neurological research terms what I have experienced as the Transcendental Moment: the rush of endorphins as the penny drops. But the closest explanation for it I've found so far is that I'm experiencing some form of Stendhal Syndrome. The phenomenon, first experienced and then coined in the nineteenth century by the writer of the same name, witnessed multiple cases of people having intense reactions to great works of art. Symptoms ranged from fainting fits to hallucinations, a rapid heartbeat to a full-blown heart attack. Admittedly my case is hardly acute, and I am over a century too late for anyone to take me seriously. And anyhow, art doesn't make me sick – quite the reverse.

Regardless of what to call it, it's moments like this experience in Paris that have compelled me to study art for so many years; to think about it and talk about it and really, really look at it. This sense of reality I know I can get so viscerally from certain artworks has dictated the direction of my life, propelling me not just from gallery to gallery but from job to job. For the best part of a decade now I have been playing hopscotch in the lower echelons of the art world; cataloguing, invigilating, valuing, selling, explaining, marketing. I'm hardly doing it for the money, and I am definitely not doing it for the clientele. I once spent the best part of a year building a professional relationship with a married auction-house client, only to have him proposition me at the end of it (and even more damningly than this, not buy anything). It was as if all our months together had been a drawn-out flirtation; the nichest foreplay of all time. I will never get back those long afternoons we spent discussing collectable fishing reels. I'm not doing it for the assurance of good art either, which is hardly a given. It's the times that it does speak to me, though – the times I am stood right in front of an artwork, locked right in – this is what I'm doing it for. I am doing it to get closer. I don't want to work in the arts, see, I want to be surrounded by them.

But the moments of pure and deep-rooted emotion that art can give me are coupled with the truth that often I feel nothing, or at least very little about it at all. It's just marks, after all. Often I find it quite offensive in all its lack. And this happens to you and me both – the lack. It's infuriating; when art makes you feel nothing at all. When you're there in person but have never been so shut out; those who get it and those who don't at that same moment existing on entirely different planes. You peer closer and the alarm goes off. They walk right on in. You won't believe you're looking at the same thing.

One spring in Naples, a couple of months before the stench of the city hangs still and weighted in the heat, I saw someone throw a broken umbrella into the rectangular void of Anish Kapoor's *Dark Brother;* both painting and seemingly bottomless pit. The thud of it reverberated around the gallery space and none of us did anything. Should you look inside today (it's not easy: you have to lean right over the glass barrier, and only when you are sure there is nobody else around) you might find, along with the offending umbrella, old boarding passes, loose change of all denominations, a crumpled receipt. On paper it's vandalism – a criminal act. But a part of me wonders whether what I saw was evidence of the work, well, *working.* Empirical proof of art making us do weird things, making us feel emotions we weren't expecting. Or instead just the opposite. Evidence of what we can be led to do when we feel nothing at all.

Take the Picasso. For the whole run up to this awed and unexpected experience, even well within my visit to the museum itself, I may as well have been asleep. It was disappointing – but nothing new. And because I never quite know what will shake me out of my dreaminess, I continue to build myself around these events. I look forward to them, spend my money and time on them, even though when it comes down to it, more often than not, it's as if my body just can't be bothered to wake up.

The moments when it does, though – *these* are the moments I can't ignore, the moments that have been at such odds with the rest of my existence. I need to find out what it is about painting that has the power to make me feel more real than if I am standing in front of someone having a conversation with them. Why is it always the paintings I remember in greater detail? How can art be more real than reality?

I have always known that reality is not a given. But still, it's nice to be backed up. Especially when it's the beacon of modern art history John Berger doing the backing. Berger tells me that reality has to be 'continually sought out'. For him, it lies beyond what he calls 'the screen' of everyday life, smashed through only by the very best of the modern painters.[1] Van Gogh put this down in writing. In a letter to fellow artist Émile Bernard, he states, '. . . the great thing is to gather new vigour in reality'.[2] I'd like to believe he was thinking of more than painting when he wrote this. And once again, Berger would agree with me. Berger was sure that van Gogh's compulsive practice was proof of his awareness of the screen between reality and himself – his work attempting always to act as a door through which he and his audience could enter into it.[3] Is this what I experienced with the Picasso: one of these portals to reality actually working? Maybe I just need to keep looking; peering into the most unexpected artworks to see if they can offer the way in, however lowly the subject. Because I would swear van Gogh's boots are more true to life than anything I've ever put on my feet. They're just right: the essential, the very essence of boot. It's transubstantiation in action. More than.

A painting like this stops us in our tracks, exuding all that was put in (the concentration, the compulsion, the obsession). A good painting demands focus, shaking everything out of our heads and making us actually look with all of our hundred percent. Could this be it? Was I so susceptible to this Stendhal-like experience in Paris because I was tired, emotionally exhausted from dealing with forty hormonal bodies? The opportunity to stand still and focus on just one thing had never felt more compelling. Art is always present, when so often we are not.

Good painting for me is something that strips whatever is depicted (an object, an emotion; animate, inanimate) right down to its essentials, scrapping all of the mishmash of information that the visual world throws at us. Digested, simplified and re-created.

Certainly, this was true for Picasso. Picasso discarded not just the visual qualities in his work, but at his most revolutionary he denied his viewers dimension, perspective and even the conventional linearity of time. Yet still we look at his work and recognise a violin as a violin; still we understand, despite the strange geometry of their faces, why he was so infatuated with his female subjects. I've often thought this is what I want of myself: to be whittled right down to what it is I'm truly meant to be. Or to exist in a world painted by Mark Rothko – colour, emotion, nothing else.

But while Picasso created a new representation of reality through art, I am searching art to find reality. Sometimes, however, the two overlap. Take cheese plants. What is it in their leaves that is so easily complemented by bold and modern brushstrokes? Their shape seems to allow for a level of abstraction that doesn't veer too far from truth. It's this adherence to truth that is one of the pivotal reasons plants like this crop up so often in modern art. Unlike a face or a body, or the sheer breadth and depth of a physical space, cheese plants already have that artistic simplicity, that *essence*. A cheese plant is just a cheese plant, and neither a child's drawing nor the coloured paper cut-out of a frail and elderly man is going to veer too far from its actual appearance. Imagine, here, Matisse as Christ, bearing these plasticky leaves and marching into the twentieth century, hailing the beauty of the flat.

It's not just in painting, art and reality can overlap far beyond the canvas. There is a track in north Tenerife that winds through banana plantations to a black sand beach. Walking down it one heat-haze of an afternoon I found it impossible to get Henri Rousseau's jungle paintings out of my head. Rousseau had never been to the jungle (had barely even left *Paris*). No matter, there was more reality in his painting than to be found anywhere along the path I was walking down. See, painting can so often be more telling, more emotive, than the thing itself. It is the world translated by another person: taking you out of your own and placing you in the shoes of somebody else. Paintings put you within the absolute context of what it is to be human.

As an intern at the Peggy Guggenheim Collection in Venice, I spent hours among the unpeopled squares and empty windows of the Italian Metaphysical painter Giorgio de Chirico. I now can't cross a piazza without a low-level sense of surreal displacement.

There are black-and-white photographs with such richness of tone
I want to lick them.

I am feeling positive. A few months after returning from Paris I decide it is undeniable that art has the power to make me feel more real. And if surrounding myself with beautiful art will cure me of this abstract ailment, then I really have nothing to complain about at all. So one weekend that winter I take the train to Ghent, Belgium, where it rains – vertically, diagonally, horizontally and incessantly. I have come to Belgium to see Jan van Eyck. *If any painter can sort me out*, I think, *he will be the one to do it*. Four hundred years before anyone invented the camera, van Eyck was doing it in oil. His portraits capture more information than an entire biography. Surely this means they will also contain the reality I am searching for.

I do not find reality at Brussels train station. On the platform a group of British men are yelling football chants in each other's faces. Everything is grey except for the vivacious purple glaze on the doughnuts in the station cafe. An enormous queue winds right out of the doorway, as if for some obscure and obligatory medicine. I imagine the bright icing seeping through the veins of our grey-toned gathering and shining verdant through our faces. On the train I stare out of a window warped with rain. Outside, a flat brown wasteland for miles. Abandoned small-holdings littered with brown-slimed garden furniture. The bare bones of poplars stark against a weighted sky.

My suitcase clatters loudly on the water-slick tiles as I walk into the minuscule city centre, where I sit on a throne under the awning of a tiny and extortionate eatery. The cafe matches the exact pink of the dress I am wearing, its excessive Rococo-Style furniture markedly more attractive than I am feeling. An elderly sweet-seller on a market stall just opposite looks at me and laughs. He had noticed me, self-consciously conspicuous with my loud suitcase, peering through the windows of every cafe doorway on the square as I'd searched, determinedly, for the perfect Belgian waffle. I'd noticed him too, recognising his stocky and smiling face as a character in an old Flemish painting. Momentarily I find myself in a place where the past is so close I could touch it; painting and reality, just as it had been in Tenerife, overlaid. Were it not for the relentless construction work going on in every street I walk down, I could be in a seventeenth-century Dutch painting. It's easy to imagine I am walking alongside grain merchants, or being jostled by rushing servants, the waterways beside us tight with boats. That's the problem with art: when reality goes astray, you never know which painting you'll end up in next.

There are short-term cures to not feeling real, and drinking is one of them. For me at least, I find that for a small period I'm all married up – my body edged with a fuzziness that matches the one inside my head. When I drink I can convince myself that sobering up will push both mind and body back into clarity; a short holiday from the actuality, where I get to kid myself that I am just having a break from the norm. That evening I find a bar decked out like a mediaeval banqueting hall. Its walls are covered with taxidermied animals, including the smiling and gaudy head of the Laughing Cow. On seeing her I have the same feeling one might when bumping unexpectedly into an old friend. It's busy, and I sit on a high stool at the bar next to two young and unattractive German men. Neither chats me up and I am relieved and offended in equal measure. It's gone midnight by the time I wander home; another anonymous figure stooped against the cold, illuminated by the light of the full moon. Buildings bow over the city's criss-cross of canals (Narcissus-like over the still black water).

As ever, the next morning the jolt back into the real via sobriety hasn't happened. Despite being ticketed, the van Eyck exhibition is so packed there isn't enough space to view the works with any sense of perspective. I am given an audio guide that beeps loudly on contact with each label. It's a Kafkaesque version of a supermarket, filled with objects that nobody will ever be able to afford. The work is brilliant. It does not make me feel real.

That same afternoon on my way back to the station, I stop off in a vintage shop and attempt to buy a T-shirt that has the word VISIONARY emblazoned across its front in huge letters. My card gets declined. Someone, I think, somewhere, is telling me something.

What have these two experiences taught me? That I can sometimes rely on great art to make me feel real, but not always? It's hardly the conclusion I was after.

When it works though, art is so much more than its materials. And it's this that makes me certain I should keep going down this route; makes me certain that, somehow, art must be the answer. It's so good for us, too – both in the looking *and* the making. By engaging the brain's neuroplasticity, making art essentially gives the brain a workout (it's been proven to help patients recover from physical traumas such as brain injury or stroke).[4] And even just viewing it does all kinds of wonderful things inside our heads.

Studying an artwork we perceive as beautiful increases the blood flow to the part of the brain related to pleasure by as much as ten percent – the equivalent of looking at a loved one.[5] By lowering cortisol (the stress hormone) and raising serotonin (the feel-good one), making and viewing art can change our outlook, and subsequently the way we interact with and experience the world. Maybe it's all in remembering this fact. That art really does improve everything.

I feel I am on the cusp of discovery. The word essence feels important here. But *how* exactly seems caught inside my chest (the moment just before a short, sharp cough). It's the same feeling as fingers tapping on the table because the word won't come. The answer's there, I'm sure of it. If only, somehow, I could bring it all together; tie mind and body to the paintings I hold close. But let's stop, just for the moment. It's time to get to grips with what exactly I'm asking, and whether or not I have company in the asking of it.

Existence is not something which lets itself be thought of from a distance, said Jean-Paul Sartre, in 1938. Except, of course, when dissociated.

II

Melancholia

I AM LOOKING at Dürer's *Melencolia I.*

Here she is. Slumped right there in the foreground, that heavy-set angel. Her dress, its pleats once uniform, falls now crumpled and ungainly around a gargantuan body. Wings seem to weigh her down – made all the worse for having the job of just the opposite (this angel is flightless, surely!). She is not alone, though she might as well be. Curled up to the left is some hybrid dog, a papery tangle of sinew and bone, and above it (attempting, perhaps, to mirror the angel but giving up halfway through the pose) a squat little cherub. Blind with boredom, it looks. A pair of feathery stubs have pushed their way through its back, aching like wisdom teeth. And all around this morose little trio, scattered mathematical paraphernalia. Tools too – nails, a saw, a wooden plank. Ladder to no known destination. Lovely view in the distance, though nobody's looking. Least not the angel. Though it *is* her eyes I'm interested in. She's got the look of someone hitting a barrier. It's that wall again. Give her two minutes today and she'd have reached for her phone. Less, even. It wouldn't have helped.

Today, melancholia might describe something like bipolar disorder. But really from antiquity until the seventeenth century it was so much more than this. Since the Aristotelian period, melancholia was perceived as something both mental and physical. It was linked to creativity, social status and intellect, but could afflict society across the broadest of its reaches – from aristocrats and intellectuals to saints, hermits and criminals.[1] Women suffered from it too, but, being women, were not allowed to enjoy any of its attributes. Our counterpart was hysteria, which made us deviant, mad and susceptible to demonic possession.[2]

People's insides were deemed far simpler back then, and the condition of melancholia was thought to be caused by an imbalance of the four stinking elements, known as the humours, that were believed to comprise each one of us – blood, yellow bile, black bile and phlegm. Symptoms could include depression (that's an obvious one – the melancholic artist has neither left us as a cultural concept, nor have we ever learnt not to fall for them), but also cholera, syphilis, stupor, lack of appetite, rage, fear, heart palpitations, sleeplessness, paralysis and seizures. Internal imbalance, yes, but melancholia could also be triggered by external events; by the general apprehension that the world itself had fallen askew.[3] It's no wonder we've turned out this way.

But it's more than melancholia that we can find in Dürer's engraving. I recognise the look in that angel's eyes because it's the look of someone dissociated.

Feel her press the sharp ends of the calliper against her thigh.

❧

'All is strange to me,' wrote Swiss philosopher Henri-Frédéric Amiel in the nineteenth century; 'I am, as it were, outside my own body and individuality.'[4] Amiel was the first to really get this feeling of dissociation down on paper. Before discovering his work, I don't have a clue that this is something I share with anyone else; these sudden blazes of feeling and the subsequent sink back into neutrality (and then again, to somewhere far deeper). Often the slip is subtle, but it can be as physical as a push. And when it's this obvious it's far easier to describe. One week it happens twice in quick succession. A shift, then again – as if something very brittle has just snapped inside me. The same abstract discomfort as scratching the surface of an unglazed vase. Or licking the skin of a peach.

Considering it was 'discovered' in the nineteenth century, research on dissociation is still in its relatively early stages. Today's statistics tell me that, in its myriad forms,[5] it affects between one and three percent of the British population.[6] Perhaps this doesn't sound like a lot, but think about it like this: that's between 650,000 and 1.85 million people existing beside/above/behind their bodies (displaced from their bodies) every single day.

And at its most extreme, it is a terrifying condition. Chronic sufferers may not recognise themselves in the mirror, may look down at their hands and not comprehend ownership. They may not be able to differentiate between dreams and something that has actually happened, or have multiple personalities – none of whom they're friends with. (A friend of mine tells me they dreamt they were possessed by the devil, and even now, days later, a small part of them is still wondering whether it might be true.) Though admittedly a community I am attempting to disentangle myself from, there is something comforting in having found one. But I believe we are far larger than this minute percentage. Dissociation, yes, is a mental health condition; but it is also something symptomatic of contemporary culture, inextricably linked to the way we live now.

See, I believe we are living through a crisis in reality.

Before going any further, it might be useful to drill down into what exactly happens in the mind when it dissociates. Far from a malfunction, dissociation is actually a protective measure stemming from the fight-or-flight response. By numbing the body to the gravity of a threatening situation, the brain minimises panic and irrational thinking, thus improving its chances of survival. Once safe, this survival measure is switched off, and brain and body will associate again.[7] And it's not only used in the fight-or-flight context – dissociation is, to a point, a natural part of our day-to-day functioning. The capacity to isolate our minds allows us to concentrate on just one thing at once. And with upwards of 10 million bits of visual stimuli hitting the retina every second, we'd get nowhere if we couldn't do this. Our brains cope with this influx of information by relying on something called lateral inhibition: the process in which one group of neurons suppresses the activity of any other that might interfere with what the brain has deemed it needs to prioritise.[8] In effect, this means that we are constantly dissociating from something or other; it is literally part of our wiring – about as human as you get. It's only when we can't snap out of it that we find ourselves with a bit of a problem. This is known as *chronic* dissociation: a constant state of dissociation that stems, as we'll see in just a moment, not just from the way we live today, but from an issue in design.

See, the high-stress situations we are likely to face today differ drastically from the ones our brains originally evolved to deal with. But although it's high time for an update, our coping mechanisms are still wired in pretty much the same way as our prehistoric ancestors.[9] This means that while contemporary stress may be caused by social anxiety, chronic loneliness or professional burn-out – long-term and psychological threats – rather than, say, the momentary and physical threat of a large predator,[10] we react to them in pretty much the same way.

And the problem doesn't just lie in the way our brains have been designed, but in something else too – in the particular characteristics of contemporary stress. On an individual basis, these day-to-day and comparatively trivial stresses might not cause too much of a concern. It's their combined and continuous effect that causes us the trouble. These two factors can cause dissociation to become a state of being rather than a temporary fix. We move away from the moment. We have tripped the switch.

You probably don't need me to tell you that this casual and consistent state of semi-stress within which many of us live our lives also has a severe effect on our sleep. With our brains constantly saying to us *You're in danger – stay alert!*, we remain unable to wind down.[11] Instead we lie in bed, staring up at the car headlights as they make tracks across our ceilings, our brains alert and waiting for a predator that went extinct 10,000 years ago.

So that's the brain – but what's going on in our bodies when we are in this state? To understand this, we have to look at the vagus nerve, the full-body network that runs like an electrical current down from our brain and through the entirety of our torsos. The vagus nerve is responsible for much of the regular functioning of our bodies, but, when chronically stressed, it will remain only half-stimulated. Heart rate, circulation and organ function will slow; blood flow will decrease; and communication will falter between the organs and brain. Our bodies can, and do, survive like this, but it's not healthy.[12]

And popping back inside the head, momentarily, we can see that repeated activation of the amygdala – the section of the brain that processes fearful and threatening stimuli[13] – makes it grow in both size and connectivity; while the hippocampus and prefrontal cortex – the important areas for memory – wither and shrink.[14] Stress literally rewires the brain.

(Perhaps one day you stared so intensely at a computer screen that the cursor somehow attached itself to your eye after you left the office. And it was hours later that evening before you managed to blink it away. This may or may not have happened to me.)

But if long-term stress can rewire the brain, it makes sense that other things can too.

Back when Dürer was alive, melancholia was cured by all sorts of extreme physical measures – flogging, bloodletting, even cauterisation.[15] I decide to self-medicate instead.

And so I begin microdosing.

Research on psilocybin, the psychoactive element in magic mushrooms, has shown unanimously the positive effect it has on depression. Even after just a couple of doses, participants' brains can remain fluid for weeks afterwards, giving them the flexibility to get out of their rut of negative thinking and see things in a new and happier light.[16] Though I've certainly felt some of my greatest moments of clarity coming down from various kinds of trips – remaining for a short while in a place less boundaried – for me it's not about depression. Dissociation and happiness are not mutually exclusive. I can be (and often am) happy and floating.

In the beginning I don't own any scales, and when I finally do buy some it takes me a long time to get around to finding the right batteries. Microdosing by eye has varying levels of success; its outcomes ranging from feeling no effects at all to attempting to work in a room with pulsating walls. Mostly though, I feel great. And in the early days, often slightly sick. Which really must prove its effect; even nausea can't lower my mood. The first time I meet my publisher in person, in the strangely formal Waterstones cafe in Piccadilly, he tells me he is curious how it had all gone with the microdosing. I judge that it may not be the best introduction to tell him I am actually on drugs right at that moment, and so agree with his chosen tense.

One Tuesday morning, sitting at my desk, I realise that the blank sheet of A4 I am looking at is moving slightly. And immediately afterwards that I have been staring at a blank sheet of A4 for quite a while now. I turn towards the window and want to climb right out of it, the outdoors looks that beautiful. That's reality. Right in every leaf, every shade of green out there. Everything the sun touches. I want to be in the grass but my landlady has organised for a man to come round and remortgage the flat. And I have emails to write. The light streaming through the window has picked up every fleck of dust its path crosses and casts dark shadows in the corners of my bedroom. The outside is so fresh and clean, I think, but I have to stay in my dirty home and live forever with the dust and the shadows and the mortgage man. Reality is through the window and I am behind the screen. Quite literally. I continue working on my emails and attempt to ignore the sheer fucking fabulousness of the light on the leaves of the copper beech outside my window. The mortgage man comes into the room and talks to me about Bristol's rising house prices and I keep sending emails. The omnipresent dust becomes more threatening every time I catch a glimpse of it. *Emails aren't real*, I think. *It's all awful in here.*

The mortgage man leaves and quite soon after so do the effects of the mushrooms. I go into my outbox to double-check that an email I'm waiting on a reply for actually sent, but can find absolutely no evidence I've been on my computer at all. I really am a lost cause if I have just hallucinated a whole morning of admin. I do realise later that I actually just needed to reconfigure my email app, and so all I have done is waste half the day. I should have listened to myself and gone out into the world instead. Which in essence seems quite the important lesson.

But does microdosing make me feel any more real? Unfortunately not. What it does seem to do, though, is lessen any kind of anxious thinking, and with that my propensity to have an existential crisis at any hour of the day. Which can only be a good thing (though not, perhaps, for this book). And in hindsight it's no wonder it hasn't gone exactly to plan. Magic mushrooms are a dissociative drug, and I hardly need any more of that. Just like ketamine and MDMA, they allow mind and body to take a few steps away from each other – which is why they're so good, in combination with therapy, for combating dissociation caused by PTSD. Disconnecting from our bodies, multiple studies have shown, allows us to explore trauma without the mind attempting to keep the body safe by blocking triggering memories and dissociating.[17] Yet though this mind–body separation can have undeniable benefits, it's not going to cure my own relationship with reality.

I am attempting to bring myself together, not increase the divide.

Meditation is also supposed to be some kind of cure. Like the microdosing, I have experimented with it in the past with varying levels of success. There have been times when, even after just a few minutes of sitting with my eyes closed, I have opened them up again into a world that bears far more clarity than it had before. As if all I needed to do was to clear some space in there to let reality in.

But first I'd like to touch briefly on its drawbacks. Dr Willoughby Britton is Associate Professor of Psychiatry and Human Behaviour at Brown University Medical School on Rhode Island. She runs something there called 'The Dark Night Project', investigating the adverse effects of contemplative practice. Her project's name was inspired by the sixteenth-century phrase 'dark night of the soul': an expression that refers to the spiritual crisis an individual can face on their journey to a full union with God. Spiritual crises span all religions and within the Buddhist tradition this rare occurrence is sometimes referred to as 'falling into the Pit of the Void'. 'It entails,' writes Buddhist meditation teacher Shinzen Young, 'an authentic and irreversible insight into

Emptiness and No Self. Instead of being empowering and fulfilling . . . it turns into the opposite.'[18] I read this on his blog. It is a transcript of a conversation he'd had with one of his students over email, and their discussion is punctuated with a cartoon outline of a figure sitting cross-legged on a black background. The speech bubble above their head says, 'It's all fun and games until someone loses an I'.

I try it out first in Pondicherry, a town on the southeast coast of India. While wandering, one evening, aimlessly down the wide streets of the city, I am gestured into a courtyard to meditate beside the grave of some guru. I say yes, though I do not know what I am doing here (I do not really know what I am doing at all). I don't know how to meditate, so I look instead at the intricately carved sarcophagus just in front of me, which feels, obviously (because it is made only of stone and corpse – and probably not much left of the latter either), dead. Afterwards, I sit alone on one of the huge slabs of rock that line the coast. The roar of the tide (it's dark, I see none of it) brings me into the present more than anything I have experienced in the country so far. Later that night in the back of my hotel wardrobe I find a copy of a novel someone had recommended to me just the day before. This may be because white people travelling in India unfailingly read and pass around the same small roster of books and have done so ever since *Shantaram* was first published, but at this point in time it feels something more telling than this. The smallest of moments continue to tether me down.

I keep saying yes until I am right up in the hills, I don't know where, being told to dance like a snake with my eyes closed. I open them. A mistake. The next morning I leave very early without anyone noticing.

I continue to say yes all the way to the furthest southern tip of the country. The day after I stay awake all night listening to someone repeatedly attempt to get into my bedroom, I watch a monk in deep conversation with a cow and a peacock. Everything bad is coupled with the best thing I think I might ever see. I stand on the beach. Nothing but water until Antarctica. Many buses later I end up in Rishikesh. The Ganges there is wide and opaque and swans through the middle of the city. Takes its time too; knows it's got a long way still to go. There is a huge wooden bridge right above it that sways ever so slightly in the wind and in my memory there's this whole flock of black birds all free-falling and flitting under and over. I remember them as ravens doing that thing ravens do playing in the wind, turning themselves over and flying upside down just for the hell of it. This may or may not be true but it's nice to have the company. When I arrive it is misty. This much I know for sure. There are boulders too, soft like the rounded shoulders of a shrug and on top of them long sheets of bright-orange material laid out to dry. Water vapour right around everywhere and it mellows everything, colours everything blue a little, as if the Ganges had flooded and receded just before I arrived. But as if it were dirty paint water, instead of dirty everything else.

I am in Rishikesh because I am in hiding. Specifically and most often around the back of the ashram I am staying in, where I smoke frantically and ignore my phone and the screaming calls of the monkeys who guard the entrance to my dorm room and drink from the taps in the dusty courtyard below it.

A few days before this I had taken a man's virginity by accident. In return he took me to a dog show attended, along with the dogs, by a host of incredibly stylish old men – all in velvet jackets, high-waisted trousers and tight white vests, with large gold medallions that hung heavy around their necks. Later we ate impossibly strong hash cakes and I ran away because I didn't know how to say no.

Unfiltered straights rip all the way down my throat.

In the ashram there is a meditation class taught by an American ex-sergeant who tells me that if I get distracted by my thoughts, I just have to stop breathing until they go away. I try to feel spiritual but I think my spirit is intimidated by her. Like a fledgling pushed from the nest too early; poorly feathered and easily stepped on. One afternoon I write all my insecurities down on a piece of paper and immerse myself with them into the Ganges. Water for purification, transformation and renewal. I go in fully clothed. Emerge ecstatic. The paper sticks onto the side of a rock just out of reach.

Any discussion of dissociation would be incomplete without bringing up technology. While it is true that I am seeking to soften the border between myself and the physical world, I fear instead that it's technology that my mind and body is seeping into (confused boundaries that leave me closer to a pixel than any blade of grass). We can already see this happening with our language; we ask each other if we have the bandwidth, and the answer is usually no. I'd said I wanted to whittle myself down, but if I do it via these means all that will remain will be my algorithms, which wasn't exactly what I had in mind. Veins run as wires while reality fades fast.

Technology exacerbates dissociation not just from ourselves but from others too. You might assume that being alive today, that existing in this global and hyper-communicative world, would have cut it out altogether, but it's really quite the opposite. Loneliness can't be cured by the technology in our pockets, and we are living in what many of today's psychologists are calling a loneliness epidemic. And as the most solitary of all the pack animals, it's no wonder we feel it so acutely. For the writer Olivia Laing, loneliness is a contradiction. 'When a person is lonely,' she tells us, 'they long to be witnessed, accepted, admired, at the same time as becoming intensely wary of exposure.'[19] Loneliness triggers a kind of hypervigilance for social threat, making the lonely individual overly alert to what they might perceive as rejection – a misinterpretation of a throwaway or teasing comment, perhaps. And it's a vicious cycle. This social paranoia makes that lonely individual withdraw further, increasing their state of isolation, which of course then goes on to exacerbate their loneliness.[20] Technology actually works to nurture this. Our phones and laptops allow us to communicate our presence through a screen, and in this way create the space for us to exist within Laing's contradiction; intense insecurity coupled with a desire to be seen.[21] It's bare-all anonymity. Existence through a screen – there it is again, that screen.

The stats show that nearly half the British population feel lonely either chronically or occasionally.[22] They make quite the gathering. Which is ironic. Unfortunately, loneliness is rarely appeased by other people. Often, when we feel it, going out into a social situation in an attempt to shake it off can make us feel alienated and far worse than if we'd stayed inside the safety of our own home (it's in cities that people are loneliest of all). And in a culture on the move, this loneliness is intensified. I find that being untethered from my usual surroundings can distance me to twice the effect. I am both away from home, and away from *home*. And it's art, again, that I think has the power to change this. It gets me thinking that maybe it was just that I was lonely, that afternoon in Paris. I was on my own, certainly, among crowds. And maybe the shock of it was something calling me, and getting through.

There's something about someone speaking to you from a hundred years ago, or five hundred, a thousand (two).

It runs further than just between our own kind. The term species loneliness describes the state of isolation and disconnection from the non-human species inhabiting the world. The Native American scientist Robin Wall Kimmerer puts it beautifully. For her, it is a 'deep, unnamed sadness stemming from estrangement from the rest of creation, from the loss of relationship'.[23] How did we become cut off in this way? As with so many things, we can blame the church.

'The great chain of being' is a hierarchical structure comprising the whole of the living (and hypothetical) world, invented by the mediaeval church and used, like some kind of ethereal caste system, to put and keep us in our places. The chain begins with God – residing over it all – and descends through angels, humans, animals and plants, right down to minerals (and underneath it all, to Hell). And it's lonely, being a human right up there at the top – especially if you're apathetic towards the existence of anything that's supposed to be above you. This hierarchy has created a real problem for us. When you tier things all up like this, how can you connect to what's below you, even respect it? And how can you stay still when the whole order of things is to climb?

The hierarchy has both accelerated and disconnected us.

But dissociation is more than just loneliness from others. It's loneliness from self.

It was all very different before God god. For many ancient and prehistoric cultures, all life existed on a single plane. We were a part of the world and equal to the rest of it; our conversation with the landscape one in which we listened, rather than told. Today though, hardly any of us can afford pets and we all speak to our houseplants. Petty attempt at dominance over the living kingdom.

Both living alone *and* working from home (though in a city, so this is despite other human presence very apparent behind each thin wall), my plants are the closest and most consistent bit of life I have to me in the everyday. Keeping plants inside isn't anything new; there's evidence of houseplant ownership from around 500 BC, and I like to think about the plants on those ancient windowsills, of terracotta vases in varying sizes (and of how all these museum pieces were once brand new). They were onto a good thing too, our ancestors. Plants are proven mood-boosters; they reduce stress levels and, research has shown, can improve daily concentration and productivity by up to fifteen percent. It's no wonder I'm one of a generation obsessed. *But this is more than just a trend*, I can't help but think, as I move the fern on my windowsill directly into my working eyeline. Along with growing numbers of those choosing vegetarian and vegan diets, it appears to me that there is a turning away from the hierarchy instilled for the last 1,000 years. In looking at something as menial as how many houseplants people are buying today (and that's disregarding the cuttings and babies we all gift and swap with each other), I find evidence of a real call, however subconscious, to go back to a more connected – a more single-plane – way of life. It's about time. But how does this link to dissociation?

Taking care of something gives us a bigger purpose, a reason to look outwards rather than in. In the same way as a painting or any other work of art, plants allow us to still, to bring ourselves together into that one moment in time; they allow a depth of contemplation otherwise rare. One life looking at another. This deep focus – or mindfulness – is an act of engagement that strong-arms me away from the passive and unembodied ways in which I so often entertain myself, like watching TV or scrolling my phone. Often at the same time. Distracted.

I am always and excruciatingly distracted. I periodically blame and delete different apps in my attempts to hinder this, but inadvertently replace the little square of blank space on my phone screen with another. There seems to be no end in sight. On the day I delete the *Guardian*, I replace my news intake by judging the political views of men on Hinge. Next I replace Hinge with Duolingo to kid myself I'm wasting time in a more productive way, but it's the same addiction at heart. A desire to tap around and swipe. I'm just like you, find myself distracting my time away; often so busy with the rest of it that feeling real takes the backseat. It's not completely our fault – these phones of ours have been designed to corrode our attention; explicitly made to grab and keep hold of it for the maximum time possible. Apple users unlock their phones an average of eighty times a day, apparently.[24] I read this online, and clicking on the hyperlink to find the original source of this stat I get taken directly to a page selling Apple products. Which says it all, really.

See, if we are so preoccupied moment by moment, we will live a whole life missing every single one of them.

Where does this distraction stem from? It's in the addiction, undeniably. But it's more than this. I think it also comes from an absolute fear of getting bored. Boredom as the enemy. I find myself judging people who stare out of the window on public transport – how can they bear to be so still; to not achieve, see, listen, constantly! How can they have wasted that small crook of time when they could have filled it up with at least thirty Instagram reels – none of which they'll remember! We are living within the antithesis of the memento mori: rather than remembering we will die, this continuous distraction works to ensure we forget all about it. And who can think of their impending demise when they are having an Alice in Wonderland-themed high tea on a London bus, or locked in an escape room, or embroiled in a city-wide version of *Cluedo* (where admittedly death is present but safe, fictionalised, and of no one you actually care about). A friend takes me alpaca walking to boost me out of a February slump. I meet one that looks exactly like me and when I reach out to stroke it, it kicks me hard in the shin.

The thing is, there is just so much to distract us.

We soak it up relentlessly, a constant barrage of information. The printing press was invented in 1439 but it's hardly been more than a century since home radio broadcasting, just under a hundred since television, and forty since the birth of the internet. Just about a hundred years, then, since the floodgates of global information were opened and the outside world smashed itself into our domestic sphere, turning our small and scattered towns into a global and globally informed community. It's the news – all of it and constantly; it's entertainment of all kinds; it's immediate and unlimited contact. It's advertising too, and social media. It's not having to wait. And it's right here, on your person or just beside you – and all at once, too; as present and uncomfortable as something stuck in your throat.

But what to pay attention to? The choice is paralysing. How can I choose how to live my life when I am immobilised even attempting to find a film to watch on Netflix? Evenings spent watching short and unmemorable trailers (perhaps, I think, I am living in one). How can any of us settle, when we know there is so much choice; a fear of missing out so deeply ingrained in contemporary culture that FOMO has been in the Oxford English Dictionary since 2013. It's not just Sylvia Plath sitting on the bough of her fig tree – we have all clambered up beside her. And though it's hard enough working out what to do with your life, having to think about who you're going to do it with is something else entirely. The options are endless: each one fitting neatly inside your phone, flat-stacked like playing cards. The same goes for Dürer's angel, surrounded by that impossible array of objects. With too many options to choose from, she is unable to make any choice at all. My Instagram feed becomes inundated with baby rabbits. I flick between these bubblegum reels and long-form news articles on the climate crisis.

We exist in a moment in history that nurtures dissociation more than ever before; a reality that not only floods us with information, but with information that is often truly terrifying. And just in the same way as our brain does when it's stressed, when our cognitive systems become overloaded in this way we tip into dissociation. This isn't necessarily a bad thing; we all need to check out every so often. But what I'm arguing is that this 'checking out' has become endemic.

(We are such complex and fragile creatures it's surprising we didn't end up the other way out: soft on the inside and with a hard-boned exterior. Sister to the crustacean. But what armour could protect us from this information that hurtles onwards, hurls itself at us at such an aggressive and alarming pace?)

So what's the next step? At this point it may seem a boundless, even impossible task. Reality – I have become aware way too far down the line (and yet told too many people what I'm doing to back out of writing about it) – is quite the abstract subject. How do I begin to write about something that only appears to exist to those who are lacking it? Is there a relevant language to even tackle a subject so conceptual? Or does reality exist in a place before language (and if so, how do I get there)?

Reality hints and hides. In truth, I fear it is a shapeshifter, something as hypothetical as a miracle. It does creep up on me though, winking at me from the Picasso postcard I keep beside me on my desk. Whatever's going on here, one of us is trying to catch the other out continuously.

And for you, as time marches on – as life becomes ever-filled and increasingly distracted – it is crucial that you stay with me on this journey. If it really is true that so many of us are living in this semi-sleepwalking state, desensitised against this constant tidal wave of information, then we need to find a long-term fix.

Ever so slowly reality unfurls in front of us, the iridescent green of an early spring fern. Let's lay this path together, make our slow way towards it.

We are living in the age of the self. Life is self-care and self-improvement. Self-harm self-affirmation self-love self-righteousness selfishness self-loathing self-absorption self-awareness self-representation, -invention and -projection. Self-fictionalisation too, but the truth keeps elbowing its way out.

III

Self

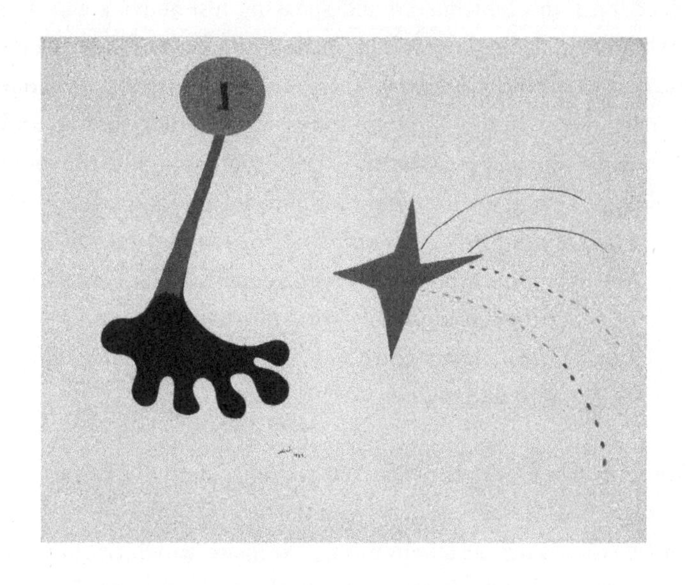

So much for the self, self, *that burr which will stick to one. I can't get it off yet.*[1]

SHELLEY
in a letter to Leigh Hunt, 1819

I AM COMPLETELY NAKED but for a pair of foam earplugs, and lying in eight square feet of body-temperature water in the basement of an ergonomic chair shop. Sitting in the cool of the waiting room just before this, I'd been listening sedately to the disembodied voices murmuring down to me. Sighs of satisfaction as customers leant back into cushions of varying firmness, the small whirs of heights and gradients being adjusted, complex payment plans and everything in tones of soft grey. The man behind the desk beside me was sitting in his own ergonomic chair. Handsome and long-haired and speaking just above a whisper; I felt relaxed just looking at him. A short time later I followed him into the small and windowless space where my session was about to take place. 'Undress,' he told me, 'have a quick shower, and then make your way into the tank,' gesturing through to the room beside us: a small nook glowing soft purple. 'And when your time in the tank is nearly up,' (seriously, softly), 'the cameras will come on.' And after a split second a sudden shout: 'No! No! I mean the lights!' He flushed, panicked. I closed the door.

I am in Bristol Float Centre and, though it pains me to admit it, I am trying to find myself.

Self moved all over the place in antiquity. For the Egyptians, Aristotle too, it was rooted right in the heart. Homer called it the *thymos* (the source of all emotions, the space to which thinking and feeling belong) and moved his to the lungs. Ancient Chinese culture placed it in the abdomen, whereas for Plato and later Galen the self lived permanently in the brain.[2] And in terms of popular belief, this seems to be where it has stayed ever since. Although scientific research has now shown that the core functions we associate with our sense of self are performed in completely different regions (namely parts of the frontal lobes and cortex, known together as the DMN – the Default Mode Network),[3] ask anyone today and they'll most likely locate their own in some central spot just behind their eyes. Sometimes I have the feeling I need someone to thud me on the head to jolt mine back into place. At others

I feel it must have strayed further, that I've left parts of it on some beach or by the side of the sink in an Airbnb and that now we're countries distant. I want mine to occupy my whole body, to steep and settle in. But first I have to find it.

It's probably worth explaining, at this point, why I have turned to the self in my search in the first place. How is self linked to reality at all? I actually think the two are synonymous with each other; if I've got nothing to feel reality *with*, how will I feel it at all? So surely if I work out exactly what my self is made up of – if I nudge it awake, feed it up and cajole it to perform – then reality will have something to latch onto when it next comes calling.

But it really is quite the money-spinner, finding yourself; it makes a privilege of all sorts of things that should be intrinsic to being a human. Like going for a walk, having a view. Breathing. Can we buy a life, a purpose; can we buy a greater reality for ourselves? We can certainly attempt it. *Oh shit,* I think. *Am I writing a book on wellness?*

The contemporary self is a capitalist structure. To firm it up, *to become more us*, we're told, we must keep buying. And so we do, hugged tight in the belief that the perfect self lies just under our skin. If only we could find the right face cream. Money sets the self, see, but this attitude is nothing new. Emily Bootle's comprehensive study on the history of authenticity highlights the attitudes of philosopher Jean-Jacques Rousseau, who stated in the late eighteenth century the importance of not only *being* who you are, but being *seen* to be who you are.[4] And with us so busy making these endless aesthetic choices to prove ourselves more real to others, it's no wonder internal reality gets put on the back burner. Even mindfulness, the practice of bringing oneself into the present moment, has been reappropriated by capitalism. In an act so ironic I'd struggle to believe it's gone without noticing, both Google and Facebook run regular mindfulness workshops for their staff (which, as you can imagine, are always full).[5]

Wellness is a 4.5-trillion-dollar industry promoting (as the Global Wellness Institute puts it) 'the active pursuit of a lifestyle that leads to a state of holistic health'. It's insane success not only strengthens the idea that we are living in a culture obsessed with 'finding itself', but posits the question of why many more of us haven't actually done so by now. Can our true selves really all be so similar? I wonder. Do they all hold a distaste for fruit bowls filled with house keys, mystery cables and a selection of uninteresting pebbles? Do they all share the same desire to stretch out across clean and empty granite surfaces, Marie Kondo-ed and languorous as cats? But then I go to the park next to my house and everyone I see is the late-millennial owner of a Labradoodle and an angry-but-well-dressed baby. Maybe it's not such a far cry to suggest that a lot of us are after the same thing.

Unfortunately for us all, wellness is impossible to actually achieve. Which of course makes it an endlessly successful industry (the cogs never stop turning, because we never actually get there). It's that hierarchy again: it's made it near-impossible to stay still, let alone go backwards. The society we have created for ourselves fixates primarily on change and growth. We'll never be able to 'get back to our roots', or 'return to the primal self' if we're always climbing. And anyhow, even if we did manage to get right down to the core, what would we find? And quite aside, for those who *do* find themselves, where have they even come from in the first place? (And wherever it is, am I there right now?)

When I first begin to consider the self, I imagine it as something fundamental: the only thing about each one of us that doesn't change at all, however much we may try. Self, in just the same way as a photograph, as something easy to capture and keep; something right at the crux of us, truer than any of the rest of it. I wonder, then, if all I need to do is peel away the outer layers to find my own; to pick myself apart like so many flower petals until there I am, the end result in this bruising process of subtraction. There I am, right down to my essence, singing sharp and true. (Petals sit in drifts around my ankles, you'd be rude to look.) And the same in good art too, remember? It's all about the essence.

But the more I learn about the self, the more I feel it can't be a permanent state. Is it instead, then, that self stays true to the body, that it mirrors the way a human being is a process (the whole bloody lot of it)? Our cells are constantly connecting, separating, reproducing, dying; the body in this sense taking on an almost operatic quality. Drama in minutiae. And in just the same way, our beliefs, attitudes and desires – all those characteristics that we believe make up the self – all of these change too. Self does not bed in. Instead, like reality, it is a flickering, fleeting thing. Like a slip of silver-blue underwater right around your ankles. Self is a thing of fluidity, a thing of flux. It is something you almost saw, but didn't.

Self can change fast and tumultuous, but this shift and fluctuation can be hard to see with the people we've known for years – the undulations; the give-and-take of that person's character over time so slow it's almost imperceptible. It only becomes obvious within a timeframe. You've met someone on three occasions, say. This interaction of yours is at such an early stage that for all you know the next time you meet could be the last (and it's only after this happens that you'll have to shift it all about in your head, add a middle and an end, rather than keep it as it was, all of it a stomach-fluttered beginning). Maybe the first couple of times you meet they are one person, but by the third they have turned into someone else entirely, and it's too early to know whether they'll switch back. (It's that moment the tone shifts, where suddenly everything feels wrong.) Or maybe you've met someone whose self is truest when you are alone together, but when out and among other people something grows between you – and even though you both keep trying to reach through, neither of you has learnt the other enough, or at all, to know how.

Despite the disconcerting feeling of listening to a song or looking at an artwork you once loved but that no longer moves you, it is perturbing how effortless it is to dismiss these changes in our own selves. Our change in character over time cannot be denied, yet is something that remains so easy to, psychologists have actually given it a name, calling the phenomenon 'the end-of-history illusion'. The term refers to this generalised idea that we exist today as we always have been and always will be; the finished product ever unchanged.[6] This attitude has some pretty historic backing. Before the Enlightenment, life, for the most part, was viewed as static. Looking at mediaeval religious imagery, with this as a consideration, the mindset is evident. Here you'll see the depiction of early Christians dressed in the same fashion as those who painted them, and inhabiting the same style of architectural space. Back then, we knew our place in the world and we stuck to it. Things changed, though, as they do, and over time new theories of history and science led us away from this stilled conclusion and to the understanding that human life and the world as a whole was an ongoing process. This was hardly a landslide reinterpretation; the full attitude shift took years. In 1859, Charles Darwin, on publishing his *On the Origin of Species*, faced backlash when he posited that animals hadn't always looked the same way. And before the big bang theory was first set down on paper in 1931, by the Belgian cosmologist and Catholic priest Georges Lemaître, scientists generally assumed the universe was completely static.[7] A startlingly visual example of this can be found many years prior in the Hebrew Bible's Book of Isaiah, in which it is written, 'All the stars in the sky will be dissolved and the heavens rolled up like a scroll; all the starry host will fall like withered leaves from the vine, like shrivelled figs from the fig tree.'[8])

I climb into the tank. In the beginning it takes a little while – though I am completely alone, and in the dark, and in the silence – to quieten everything going on in my head. To get to just my heartbeat, my breathing (which is louder, messier, than I had anticipated). I have the distinct and disconcerting feeling that there are many people floating in here with me. Not many of them I'd want to see me naked either. And vice versa. My head feels like a railway station: coffee spilt all over the floor, smokers loitering around the exits. The Tannoy won't shut up and all the trains are late. It's no wonder. Each one of us is filled with other people, our selves both tempered and buoyed.

But it's not just other people who fill our heads up. The science writer Jo Marchant tells me that rather than inheriting a single biological self from our parents, our genes encode all sorts of potentials. The social environment each of us is born into, along with our ongoing experience and relationship to the wider community, help to determine which of these selves we become.[9]

Self, like life, is all just down to serendipity. This makes it fragile as hell, something as easily bolstered as it is breakable. (Self as chance, more than anything.) And, just like the body (like a hunch, or a nervous tic, or legs wide or crossed or jittering), self shifts not just according to where we are in life, but who we are with. Comments, too, can change the trajectory. They settle deep in our minds, the roots from which the rest of us grow. Those that take can spread disproportionately, suffocating anything around them like ivy or bindweed. Insults are often more long-lasting than compliments; the latter working best when repeated. Still, it only takes a few bad words to smother a whole garden of them. See, if we've not got the right people around us, having the right self is near fucking impossible. They take up home in our heads and will not leave.

It's exasperating, how delicate we are in all this. Licked into shape like bear cubs (formed and again from every angle).

A further theory on self posits that each of us has several sub-selves, each one dedicated to a different activity. (One, for example, to creating and building on friendships; another for the professional sphere; and yet another for finding and keeping a mate.) As we've already seen, our brains are coping constantly with an unceasing wallop of information – making dissociation, on some level, necessary for our successful day-to-day functioning. And this endless act of prioritising makes the subself crucial, with the brain letting only one part of us take the wheel at any given time.[10] It's like Walt Whitman said: 'I am large, I contain multitudes.' We are a many-authored book.

I have many names, too. At least, I call myself a multitude of variations on the name Francesca. It changes with each address, profession, new acquaintance, boyfriend. I compartmentalise and allow no fusion. It's gone on for years and has become an increasingly tangled web, especially now everyone appears to be relocating to Bristol. Years ago, when I moved to London to begin my MA,

I decided to rebrand myself as Cesca. The C (never before capitalised) felt alien and vulnerable: like a night creature unexpectedly out in daylight, blinking and shy. When someone first asked how to spell it in an austere and strobe-lit classroom I had a momentary blank and my reply came out as a lilting, faltered question. That was pretty much the end of Cesca, though she does crop up every so often and most recently I found myself using her solely on first dates and hookups. This is a separation between my public and private life that I know cannot be healthy. Francesca is often only for work, and I use Fan – a childhood nickname which I guess just stuck – for family, close friends and anyone I want to really know me (and, in an accidental moment of bare-faced vulnerability, my landlady). I am Fran for everyone else, though I did not choose this. It can go either way, see, someone shortening your name; an act both intimate and aggressive. To shorten someone's name without asking is a taking and a snapping of a thing that's not theirs to break; a disposal of someone else's belongings. For years Fran reminded me of school, and whenever I heard it I visualised my year nine chemistry teacher. The name sounded sterile in her mouth and made me feel ugly. Sometimes I want to be an Effy or a Fay: light and pretty names that wear floral dresses and ride around on bikes with wicker baskets. Not a name that stomps around New York in heavy boots. Fran is a footstep, I feel a wisp.

I have, however, known them all for a long time now, and would feel curiously sad for any of them to die out. So I keep all afloat, rebalancing the difference with each new person I meet, moderating myself as to who I've decided to be at that particular moment. I start dating a man who doesn't quite know what to do with his own and so when we are together, we go without. It is inappropriately intimate, as if we've skipped to a shared future with neither of us really sure how we got there. A place beyond names (though we know little else about each other to supplement the loss). One evening he stays over and we wake in the heaviest part of the night. Sleep has split me into six, my self all a fracture; all about the room and beyond it. A necessity, perhaps, in each of our many contradictions, for the parts of our selves that don't get along to find breathing space; to shuffle through the fallen leaves and the street litter under ceaseless orange glare. While we sleep on, unaware. But touch can be a rallying cry, calling us back from wherever we've got to. We find each other, blindly.

Here I am without sound, without clothes, neither hot nor cold. Nor much sense of gravity, either. There are two raised shapes on one of the walls. One red – a panic button that will alert reception in case I have any momentary disasters; and the other grey, which turns the lights on and off. I reach out to the grey one. The darkness is immediate and total. I lie still. All distraction erased. Stripped down right to the knuckle in a space that might be infinite.

My body falls to the hold of the water. Brain follows suit: its waves shifting states from beta (waking awareness) to alpha (deep relaxation). And then another shift, from alpha to theta (the state of our brains just before falling asleep, and when we are dreaming).

A short while passes before I realise that the darkness above me has begun to break up into wisped clouds. I am looking down on a thick green forest. It strikes me that I am flying. Later, after some other period of nothing, my perspective shifts. Now I find myself flat against a city pavement. Strong sun directly overhead, so all I can see are the foreshortened silhouettes of people walking right over me. Suits and briefcases and long-handled umbrellas hurry past. Must be rush hour.

Hallucination within the context of sensory deprivation is relatively common. Our brains, as we already know, have been designed to pay attention to everything going on around them. With all stimuli eliminated, the mind falls into a state of deep relaxation, releasing vast quantities of endorphins and making whatever it was I was seeing a kind of waking dream. But something else is going on here. This highlights as much a pattern of behaviour as the headspace I was in. I have an innate urge to be distracted. In this context, with no commands needing to be sent out, the logical parts of the brain begin to match the pace of the creative ones. Not knowing what to do with itself without sensory stimulation, it begins to make it all up.

I think later of Leonardo, who would study peculiar shapes and marks in rocks and invent imagery right out of it. Miró, too – when he had first arrived in Paris in 1919 and was too poor to properly feed himself – would lie on his small bed staring at a ceiling damp and stained, semi-hallucinating from hunger. Strange objects and creatures would emerge, dancing across his vision and end up immortalised in his early work.

Self is not something concrete, we know this much by now. But how about this? Instead of something transient either (something that changes states like water), is it that self is a thread? Does it run through every single moment of our lives, weaving together this complex tangle of memory, dream, opinion and desire we all keep inside of us – does it tie it all together like a well-composed painting? If it is a thread, it's no wonder we've got to where we are today. (Because if it is a thread, it's no wonder that sometimes it gets tangled, that sometimes it snaps.)

Self then, as biographer, forming narrative out of chaos. Here we all are, attempting to firm up and promote our own stories. We display ourselves, all of us, as things that are logical. As if.

These tales of ours (great epics written in blue Bic) are infinitely more than the body, but the self does live within its bind. The body makes the self physical, however insecure we happen to be about it. Makes me think of the embarrassing expanse of William Blake's figures. How their size doesn't make them strong or powerful but quite the opposite: gives them instead more of a soft and fragile mass to injure and upset. Not god-like, just subject to huge emotions. With the body in tow it's tricky to set down one's current self and pick up a new one; near-impossible to change the narrative. But self *without* the body to constrain it, the self online, this can be something else entirely. To exist without having to pander to its everyday needs, in waves of energy or data. In the unseen. (Things might just have been easier if instead we all could have been birds, or a cloud. Or nothing at all.)

None of us need reminding that social media is bad for our mental health. But it's not just making us feel worse about ourselves, it's making us feel less real. Bound up as we are in this loud and lonely era, our tiny (yet *important!*) personal narratives fly all the way out through the ozone layer. Here, just for the moment, they find themselves gravity-less – bouncing about in the great void before ending up back in front of the eyes of our friends, acquaintances, professional contacts and crushes. The longed-for and the loved. Shakespeare was wrong. There is an answer. We are so full of promise and despair.

Online, it's easy to curate a fictional self-image. Online, says Olivia Laing, 'you have the chance to write yourself into the person you want to be and to imagine others as you wish them to be, constructing them for your purposes'.[11] She could be describing a bad date: that first meeting less a hello than a goodbye to the person you'd crossed your fingers for; a strange sense of loss felt for someone who existed only in your head. There you sit across the table from one another in a pub you know your friends aren't likely to be at, polite with your drink and your small talk. Disappointment sitting damply between you (evident even on the approach).

Social media allows us to take artistic licence with the self. It's here we shine it up and put it on a pedestal; each one of us a product of our own marketing. This is exhausting – a relentless contradiction (you want to be free, but you can't stop selling yourself). We're all of us like those portraits that have been copied and copied because the subject has only ever sat for one artist. So, all the way down the line – in this family tree of poorly rendered clones – although the likeness remains apparent, the distance from the sitter is so great, each is really an image of someone else entirely. 'People want the idealised image,' says the writer Susan Sontag, 'a photograph of themselves looking their best. They feel rebuked when the camera doesn't return an image of themselves as more attractive than they really are.'[12] And with image a far cry from self, we find ourselves on troubled ground. Since the invention of the camera in 1816; or the invention of mirrors many years and miles distant; or, even earlier than that – since the first prehistoric being first happened upon their image in a body of water – our sense of reality has become skewed. Since this point in time, as well as doing, we have been perceiving ourselves doing it. This self-awareness has led, over so many years, to a sense of removal: a split between self and self-image. We are somehow displaced. Our use of social media exacerbates this discrepancy, widening the gap between who we are and who we think we are.[13] Today, the self fades with each photo we upload: the camera making one a tourist, as Sontag tells us, 'in other people's reality, and eventually in one's own'.[14] And if it really is true that we sit one degree of separation from ourselves, how are we supposed to fully connect to anyone else? And how are we supposed to set ourselves down in the world, to feel it fully?

I'm in my early thirties. The sliding door years. You've been around for just long enough to look back at all the options you didn't take, branching off into alternate pasts like cracked ice. I keep meeting people I'm sure I could have been. Which I'm aware sounds impossibly narcissistic – but these days, aren't we all? This is a narcissism that's been nurtured from birth, tying into an assumption held since the seventies that children need high self-esteem to grow into professionally successful adults.[15] Unfortunately, for the last fifty years, rather than self-esteem, narcissism has been flourishing instead.

It was really the nineties, with the birth of reality TV, that narcissism became part of the mainstream. Me and you grew up in full belief that anyone could become a somebody – even us![16] Use of social media has spiralled these narcissistic tendencies out of control. Here we are, each one of us a walking brand; a positive affirmation on legs because we can, and don't we know it! But when all the successes or experiences we have been told will fall into our laps, don't quite happen – when we realise that we can't actually 'be anything we want' – our selves as they are come to some kind of disconnect. We find ourselves surrounded by the people whose lives we'd thought would be our own, but with no idea how to make it that way. With our expectations unmet, our brains fall into an uncomfortable cognitive dissonance,[17] and we are left having to work out how the hell to reconfigure ourselves.

This becomes clear to me when very early one morning I am cycling across Bristol after spending the evening with a man who had a framed photograph of himself with his ex on his bedroom wall. It was the kind of night that's a troublemaker (puts everything in place to get you to imagine loving someone, and then pushes you right out just as you do). It had been hot that day – impossibly so – and we'd lay, all wrapped up in each other, in the park until late. Under a meteor shower too, and when I cycled home across the night there was the blaze of one still seared right into my vision. How it was all there and then gone without explanation. One of those nights. The moon was right on the cusp, huge and peach-coloured. The same texture too, somehow.

Anyhow, a few hours later that same morning I am driving up into the great and moody hills that mark the border between England and Wales. I am on my way to a first birthday party, yesterday evening tilting about inside me as I veer down the tiny lanes. I am still filled up with the night – the long cycle home and the picture of his ex and how sex can sometimes make you feel sad and how I had this sense that I'd lost everything, though nothing had even yet happened. And when I arrived I saw it. There it was, under a gazebo in the front garden. By little more than my fingertips, there was the reality I'd almost grasped, the self I had imagined would be my own. I drink too much rosé and look at the babies; my own and very current reality – spiked and confused – overlaid on the one I am in. Softer. More blanketed. I guess it's this kind of moment that makes you feel that self must be a real prominent thing. I find myself unable to shift gears; am right on the edge of things, peering in. And something inside me, far away from anything rational, shifts slightly. I feel all of a sudden very much in my thirties.

The lights do, indeed, come on. I rub a hand right across my face. Epsom salt concentrate burns into my eyes. I may have gone gently into the night, but I come out of it swearing and stumbling half-blind into the shower.

Floating, if not allowing me to entirely lose my sense of self, has made me realise how many selves there are inside me: all kinds of people vying for my attention, and all of them I seem to have given a home inside my head. And though at points my brain was desperately coming up with all kinds of ways to distract me, after I left the tank these voices were quieter, far quieter, than they had been for a long time. I leave the floatation centre and sit for a while in the dried-out park just across the road. Everything is bright, and for some time I feel each dried leaf, each blade of grass, minutely. If I couldn't hear my own breath I would have forgotten, I think, that there was anything inside of me at all. I am a body, and little else. And it makes me wonder, in the gentle headspace I find myself in, whether reality might be found in the body instead; that maybe it's all in the feeling rather than the thought.

It's time for us to connect with reality in a far more physical capacity. Clamber up onto the high board and dive right on in.

IV

Touch

SOME TOUCH IS MORE REAL than others. Sometimes it's good to be pressed. Or pinched. I like bruises, the silvered down inside a broad bean pod, and the thick green warmth of tomato plants. Stubbed toes, and anything on the shin – both these things are more real than closed windows and central heating.

There's biting your lip too, or somebody else's; and the feeling of gravel being picked out of your knees with tweezers, sat on one of those grey plastic school chairs in some village hall you can no longer remember the name of. Cycling barefoot and missing the pedals: the shock of scraping the ends of your toes along the gritted tarmac (the hot day maybe has melted it all into thick sticky bubbles and your toes are sharp-scraped and covered in black). And maybe you can feel that in your feet when you're reading this, like I can in the writing.

Someone I speak to on a dating app asks me if I think the contemporary cure for melancholia might be BDSM. I wonder out loud whether I am only dating to publicise my work. Reality is a conversation starter though. Everyone has an opinion on it and most of the time it gets me laid.

❧

When I first started thinking about reality in the very early stages of this book, my little sister told me about an old colleague of hers who was missing a finger. It had never felt like a part of his body, he'd said, so he'd just picked up a kitchen knife one evening and cut it off. I sometimes think about how many attempts this would have taken. Whether he'd had to trick his body into doing it before his mind had a chance to catch up. And I wonder if, the moment he'd done it, he couldn't quite believe it had happened, and if he ever regretted it. Most of all I wonder what he did with it, the finger. That maybe he buried it somewhere in a shoebox like you would a dead guinea pig. Or did he keep it as a relic: the same as a shard of bone in the back of a signet ring, or a lock of plaited hair? Even with it gone, he might have continued to feel it. Some people's missing limbs remain viscerally present, a phenomenon caused by the neurological maps we each have of our own bodies.

Our brain's preconceptions of its own physical boundaries can get confused with amputation, causing chronic pain in empty space.[1] That's reality going in the wrong direction. Best get rid, some say. The Transhumanists would certainly agree. Without the body, this dystopian lot would tell us, the self can be anything but. 'You can be anything you like,' they say, 'you can be big or small... lighter than air, and fly; you can teleport and walk through walls. You can be a lion or an antelope, a frog or a fly, a tree, a pool, the coat of paint on a ceiling.'[2] As if the body were something we could all shed in the same way a snake; shimmy it off and discard. As if we were in ours only fleetingly, and perhaps tomorrow will hop over into something else. Just wherever the fancy takes us. Hermit crabs, the whole lot of us.

Bodies bring about all kinds of problems, and ours are sometimes easier to forget about than to inhabit. It's not that some of us live in ours unthinkingly – the problem lies in living *too* thinkingly. The body doesn't deal in words, see, and on realising this it suddenly makes sense to me why the cures for melancholia are so physical (and moreover, why I never had much of a chance of finding reality through my research-heavy exploration into self). It's about bringing yourself out of your mind and right back down to it; filling yourself out with reality, right to the inside edges of your fingertips. It's about making the inside conscious. Although the body doesn't deal in words, language *is* important on the eyes. As we explored in the last chapter, just one comment can transform who we are entirely; but, more than this, it also transforms what we see. Use changes the body too. I fall in love or lust and see my own as an object of desire. Some mornings I wake up impossibly heavy, or so light I could spiral away into nothing. Or I stop having sex and my body becomes stolid and practical and nothing else.

On one hot and listless day, I leave my city and take a train to Hastings to visit a nudist beach. The woman behind the tourist information counter looks me right in the eye and warns me of the debauchery I will find there. This could not have been further from the truth. A colour-wheel of pinks laid out against a flat expanse of beige and grey. Stone, sand, water, an array of worrying-looking moles. Nothing else under endless blue sky. It's only when I lie down and make myself comfortable on the sand, across the beach from where the nudists are spread like seals over the rocks, that I realise it hadn't been the gaze I was yearning for after all. I think I wanted instead to put my naked body into a new setting. I wanted to take it on holiday, give it a good time. Let it be touched; if not by someone else, then at least by the water. By air that tastes of salt. After a numbing swim a middle-aged man wearing just walking boots and a hat strolls over to talk to me for a long time about his dog. I sit up and he stands closer, crotch level with my face.

It's difficult, near impossible, to inhabit something that doesn't have an objective form. Except. Except when the body is an object in itself. And this is what makes drawing such a good way to understand it. The forced contemplation of drawing, by whichever means, allows the body to be viewed as object, and by the same principle, as objective. When I think of the body I often think of Iggy Pop. In 2016 he posed nude at the New York Academy of Art. Studying these drawings I find him more insubstantial on paper; less a tangled string body and more an ending, each study the fine and fragile resting place of all that violent exhibitionism (the pent-up energy of a trapped and wild animal). Because although it's true we *see* the body objectively when we draw, it doesn't always end up that way on paper. This is the brain's fault. Constantly building on information it's stored up from past experience, the brain integrates whatever it's looking at with prior knowledge of what it already knows about that particular thing.[3] Anyone who has been to a life drawing class may find they can particularly relate; it's far easier to draw the body in your head than the one you have in front of you. And to be the body in your head too. None of us really know what we look like, see. And nor does what we look like have much at all to do with who we are inside. Although we do, as we know, exist within its confines, the body is more, as Paul Klee would say, 'than its exterior presents to our eyes'.[4] And the same goes for objects. I think back to Picasso's still life; how that jug was more human than anything ceramic. In life as in painting, the body often isn't at all about what we see.

Photographs don't help with the knowing, nor mirrors. Although they *can* capture the same fleeting qualities as a self-portrait – a split-second glimpse at the weather that plays continuous across our faces. In a mirror we may find ourselves composed and beautifully framed: captured into two-dimensionality, if only for a moment. It's rare, though, to catch yourself in one unawares, without recalibrating your face to fit the mood (or the one you would like to appear in, anyway). Although you can catch yourself out, this is rarely a good thing. (Maybe you are sitting in the backseat of the car and spot yourself in the rear-view mirror. Something is off. A moment later you realise you are looking at a reflection of your mother.) Sometimes a reflection can hinder the self. You want to be expansive but the mirror translates this desire of yours in completely the wrong way (perhaps there are whole days in which you feel huge, unable to fit through door frames or taking up the entire width of the pavement).

So often the body is not the body we had in mind. It changes constantly, but never quite transforms as we might wish. And so it's no wonder we make it up (and edit it down). It seems to me that there are two bodies; the outward one a whole different animal from the one we actually inhabit: shape-shifting with every mood, every reaction. I am tall, which when commented on (it is always commented on) is very often prefixed with the word lovely. Only one of these things is always true. Small men feel the need to comment on me when I am out in public. As if they have never looked up before and seen something quite as big as five foot eleven.

The body I inhabit today, and yours too, I imagine, is built on these passing comments. Shoulder blades with a different history to hip bones, freckles dedicated to someone else entirely (it's words that sew us together, remarks that act as needle and thread). Same in the Italian Renaissance. Here, artist training was a formulaic venture and drawing the nude was no different: a patchwork of disparate body parts sourced and spliced together to make some kind of a whole. Renaissance drawing treatises gave rules of perfect proportion that essentially enabled an artist to draw from life without ever actually having to look at it. This was a reined-in version of natural variety that fitted neatly between the pages of a book. There were drawing manuals to share around: pages of printed body parts you could slot together on your surface until you had yourself a human. Articulated wooden figures, contemporary casts and antique sculpture. Inspiration gained also from other artists, from the student sat next to you in the workshop, from frescoed churches or private and palatial homes. Perhaps from your own close-held memories too; each one a painting in itself. The curve of a back in chiaroscuro, contours slowly illuminated in a dawn the colour of milk (Vermeer's mornings; more a quietness than anything else). All of this feeds onto the canvas; has been calling to us for some five hundred years now. Reminding us of that one moment, that single touch.

Donatello is an artist who really understood touch. Hands roam everywhere in his work. Pulling, gripping, caressing, clawing. Chubby, grasping fingers. And as well as flesh, every other imaginable texture rendered exquisitely in terracotta and marble. In one relief the Virgin and Child are at rest, nose to nose. In another they gaze out with two sets of unblinking almond eyes, faces close and cheeks touching, and I can't help but imagine the warmth in-between. The wet hot stick of it. Each relief immortalises a moment so intimate it seems almost wrong to look. There is one sculpture, terracotta and in the round, where a finger grazes (just!) the child's toes. You've never seen something so unconscious set down like that. Next – and much later in the story – a lamentation in relief. One angelic hand rests flat-palmed on the dead body of Christ. Cold to the touch, it looks like. Or did the artist capture the moment just before death fully sets in? And if this is the case, then has he left the angel with perhaps the last traces of human warmth? Let's hope so, for all our sakes. In the same marble panel there's another angel; one hand at Christ's brow and the second smacked hard against their own grieving face, covering skin and hair and squashing the bridge of their nose. Hot tears collect in their palm.

Later – towards the very end of the sixteenth century, when drawing from the nude had started to become commonplace – models would pose as classical sculpture; the body as a vessel for fantasy, arranged to replicate someone, or some*thing* else entirely. We share this artistic licence in our image making today. Living in a culture that has normalised the fictional presentation of the body, we present our own as a lie. It's no wonder we don't feel at home.

But to go back to the question in hand, how can we feel real in our bodies if we don't know what our bodies look like? And even more problematic, what happens when we have nobody to observe, to feel, or to experience our bodies for us? Touch, so said the French philosopher Denis Diderot in the eighteenth century, is 'the surest knowledge of external bodies in their substantial reality'.[5] Touch is the great connector, allowing us to perceive, bodily, the exactitude of our physical contexts. And when we lack the opportunities to learn and experience through our bodies, or manipulate the world around us with our hands, it takes on a level of abstraction.[6] Our surroundings become somehow distant.

The pandemic of 2020 and concomitant national lockdowns absolutely affected our relationship with the body. In the isolation experienced by so many of us, how could we be expected to know we were any more real than a drawing? The COVID years exacerbated every one of the issues that make up the wall of dissociation that I am attempting, through this book, to smash through. Loneliness, without doubt; and excess screen time too, a remove from the strictly physical. But something else stopped happening for a lot of us – touch. For over two years we had to completely reconfigure our relationship with it. Touch became something that made us recoil, it was to be sanitised and protected against. This was a time when not even the air between our bodies was a safe zone. And for this reason, this strange era where it was out of bounds, for so many of us touch became something we wanted more than ever (though just as bad as not being touched was being touched by the wrong person; stuck in the same place with the only available option never less appealing).

And so it makes sense then, that the summer of 2021, the summer in which the UK was tentatively opening back up, was billed by the media as the Third Summer of Love. People needed this again completely; we were skin starved and touch hungry, a whole crowd desirous of a reconnection with our own bodies and the bodies of others. Capitalism, as ever, leapt on board. Those post-lockdown months saw a notable acceleration in sales of sex toys, lingerie and condoms. Sex parties lost their sense of taboo and everyone I knew became polyamorous. It was during that time that a friend of mine was meeting somebody just to get tickled by him, and another had realised all she wanted from another person was to be touched, all over and continuously. To have the very outlines of her body delineated. It was desire laced with danger, which made it all the more tantalising. And all of us who'd spent the last two years avoiding it, finally caught COVID.

Dating apps helped in this strange period. Because we all lost our social skills for a bit. Where I live, the app men are small and kind-looking and have all proudly scaled the summit of Pen-y-Fan. On the way to the top (pulling each other up hand by soft-skinned hand) they share words of encouragement and whiskey out of a flask. Positive affirmations echo around the valley. I think they must have been bred like pheasants and released into the city's allotments. They make their own beer and play board games and their dream dinner party guest is always David Attenborough. Which must be exhausting for him. I let them lie dormant inside my phone while I search elsewhere for someone to spank me.

Dr Brad Sagarin runs a lab in Illinois that researches the neurological effects of BDSM (Bondage and Discipline/Dominance and Submission/Sadism and Masochism). The front page of his website, *The Science of BDSM*, has a photo of the whole team wearing matching black leather waistcoats. Power imbalance, both physical and psychological, is at its heart, and Sagarin writes about something known in the BDSM community as 'subspace': the altered state often experienced by those taking a submissive role in a D/s (Dominant/submissive) interaction. Participants in this state share a feeling of heightened awareness, of living outside of past and future time constraints and instead existing in the here and now – many of the same cognitive benefits, in fact, as meditation. As an activity that requires intense focus, participating in BDSM forces people to pay attention to nothing but that particular moment. And in the same way as meditation, it is a way of bringing oneself *inside* the moment, rather than constantly considering what will happen in the next one. (Tangentially, many people describe their experiences within BDSM scenarios in religious or spiritual terms – a feeling of oneness with the universe, mind-expanding, transcendent and uber-connected:[7] all signature traits of mystical or religious experience.)

This is something we might also call the state of flow: those moments you can be nothing and nobody and nowhere else. For some this can be BDSM, for others climbing, surfing or even putting together Ikea furniture. And for yet more people this state of flow can be found through making art – any skilled and physical practice that connects you both with yourself and to the world outside your head. With a pure focus on the body, the state of flow is associated with a temporary reduction of activity in the DMN (the part of the brain thought to contain our sense of self).[8] So is it that the self is actually *juxtaposed* with reality? Is it only when we quieten it right down that we can fully immerse ourselves into the real? It makes me think about the times I have been so struck by particular artworks, and whether it was that I couldn't look away because I had found myself inadvertently locked into somebody else's flow.

But let's head back to the bedroom, momentarily. When we lose ourselves in the pure sensation of something, we also lose all the up-in-our-head stuff that distracts us away from it. In other words: with everything we lose, we gain space for a feeling of reality. I do not find it difficult to source research partners for this section of my book, and breaking up my day with casual sex becomes one of the myriad reasons I enjoy working from home. There's something about living within a strict set of physical rules (even for just an extended lunch break) that forces me into the present, and I find in these moments an immediacy that far overrides everything else I experience during my working day. My self quietened and my body in all its capacities never as evident. This is nothing new. Sex manuals like the ancient *Kama Sutra* and eleventh-century *Koka Shastra,* as well as the fifteenth-century Arabic *Perfumed Garden of Sensual Delight,* all recommend a degree of physical pain as a necessary part of good sex.[9] But pain (within the context of sexual pleasure) doesn't seem to be the end result here. It's something more than this – extreme sensation as yet another way of bringing oneself into the body, another way of feeling real.

In 2016, a comprehensive study was made on the non-suicidal reasons that people self-harm. Time and again, subjects interviewed brought up the boundary-defining qualities of such a physical act – its 'wakening' effect.[10] To feel pain is to make you realise that you exist as a body right at that moment in time. Focus on the self is replaced by attention on the immediate present and on physical sensation alone.

It's the same with love. Falling in love can bring you back to yourself, ushering you into the real through the sheer force of somebody else's focus. Love makes a work of art of us all. Years ago, in an invigilating job where each minute ached with boredom (the kind of work that puts you in a soupy state of mind), I ran my fingers right over the bronze ridges of a Constructivist sculpture. It cut through the day's shapelessness like a knife through butter; I swear I'd never wanted anything so much. I can still feel it on my skin, that particular touch, all along the fingers of my right hand (touch as memory – that's a different subject altogether). The sculpture wasn't quite love though – more akin to lust, I think. I was sated, in a way impossible with love.

But as ever, the balance can tip the other way. Touch can be something unwanted. And so often is. The feel of a hand on your body can remain, sometimes even for years afterwards. Crucial movements like Black Lives Matter and Me Too have brought this to the fore – unwanted touch as tied to power structures and historic oppression. Late for a meeting, I yelled D*on't touch me!* at a man on the tube who pulled me backwards by my bag in the queue I was attempting to bypass and I felt the immediate power in the words. He jumped back, defenceless. And sex, too. Sometimes sex is an arbitrary event: it might or it might not have happened (though it usually did, nonetheless). Sometimes you forget it because it was never worth remembering in the first place, and other times you work hard to because it's something that sits so uncomfortably with the rest of you, it's really the only way to carry on.

They're all over the place, once you get to looking. Tender bodies dragged off by marauding troops, leered at by ancient and lecherous men and groped by all manner of gods and monsters. Their entire character is to succumb. And to anything too, if the myths are to go by. To beautiful white bulls (flowers entwined around their horns), and to heavy mists and to swans and to small men with the legs of a goat. They loll about, these women, accepting of the inevitability that their egg-white bodies have led them into. Hard to relate to this behaviour unless it happens to you. And when it did, to me, I didn't struggle either, not really. I did, actually, exactly what has been painted for the last five hundred years. I stayed still, waiting for it to be over. Whatever your presence on this earth – whether your body exists as slow-fading marks on a canvas, or instead in the half-dark of your own bedroom – it's the same. You dissociate.

And it's only far later, wandering the jewellery-box rooms of the Palazzo Borghese in Rome, that I come to this realisation about these paintings. See, I'd always questioned why women were so rarely depicted as we actually are – powerful, vicious things. In part we can translate this disparity as a patriarchal dismissal: visual evidence of an endemic imbalance of respect and power. But this aside, and on a purely aesthetic basis, surely it would have been more dramatic to show a bit of back and forth? I struggle to look at the work set upon the walls of this golden space, and am quietly furious that the casually exerted dominance of one man over a decade ago has suddenly made me unable to look at the paintings I used to love. And at the same time I am deeply unsettled that for this many years too, I have been looking at images of rape without question, and that I have been led blind to believe that this is what beauty is.

As an aside, it would be easy to explain this away, to tell myself that this is the exact and only reason for my dissociation. It's not. I've felt dissociated for most of my remembered life. There are, and we've already spoken about this, certain things that can exacerbate dissociation, and this kind of trauma is obviously one of them. I was not alive in the fifteenth century, but if I was, I might believe that any one of the four bodily humours could be ignited by this kind of sudden and awful shock. The remains of the inner fire when cooled would resemble black coals, taking on the characteristics of melancholy – a cold, dry humour. This blaze, as stated by the Florentine Humanist Marsilio Ficino in the same century, could instigate a frenzy of artistic activity, but it wasn't to be recommended. Afterwards, acrid smoke would fill the body, drifting up to the brain, where it would cause depression.[11] Thinking too much could do this too: drying the brain out, extinguishing the body's natural heat and consuming its resources.[12] I guess I really always was set to veer towards melancholia in one way or another.

In the midst of my unexpected research trajectory, I take a group of students to a grand Palladian palace in the Veneto. Villa Barbaro is decorated with mid-sixteenth-century frescoes by the artist Paolo Veronese. All sorts of people gaze down from the ceiling as we slide about the glossy floors in huge protective slippers. The *piano nobile* (main floor) is a small space but one made confusing with the inclusion of illusory doors and ornate marble balconies, flanked each side by Corinthian columns. Pastoral scenes replete with ancient ruins compete with the flawless gardens just outside. On entering, we find the whole family at home, set among the gods and the household pets. It is a bizarre menagerie, with hunting dogs that skulk amidst monkeys and flower-laden swooping putti. Scuffles both mortal and divine. Above us sits the goddess Diana. Caught in a moment of exceptional tenderness, she is nose to nose with one of her dogs, its paw resting lightly on her thigh.

In the next room, a servant peers out from behind a half-closed door, hat in hand and his face a polite question. 'Who are you?'

he might be asking. 'Why have you knocked, expecting to be invited inside?' It appears, in fact, that you already are. Musicians stand monumental in painted alcoves: a play on the solid gold and marble statuary that peers out from behind the columns. And the statues are also a trick on the eye, a depiction of the three-dimensional in flat and painted in all the patterns of exotic stone. Each figure has been illustrated poised with their chosen instrument – flute, mandolin, tambourine, trumpet, harp, clarinet, violin. It should be quite the cacophony, but the museum guards seem to have shushed even those who happen to exist now only in fresco.

Next to two figures in sky-blue silk (fabric so starched you'd be hard-pressed not to hear it crunch) there sits a small orange and white spaniel. Perhaps the dog is the owner's own, five hundred years dead by now. Disconcertingly, its exact replica is busily trotting about the gardens outside – as if the skill of the artist was so great that his frescoes had peeled themselves from the plaster and escaped. No such freedom for one figure I found, though. In the Room of the Oil Lamp there sits *Virtue Restraining Passion*. The latter is a woman in green, her head pulled to one side at an awkward angle. The imploring gaze of Virtue, directed by the cane he holds in his left hand, points upwards. Hers, determinedly down. She is evidently in trouble for something, as she's been depicted wearing an instrument of punishment known as a scold's bridle. The horse's metal bit is firmly placed between her teeth.

I realise I'm finding myself drawn towards objects that throw me right back at myself. The tortured sinuosity of Mannerist sculpture. Screaming Baroque. The wretchedness of Masaccio's *Expulsion*. The paintings of Francis Bacon too, art as an assault for every one of our senses – the taste, sound and smell of them.

Paintings that make you want to throw up on the floor of the gallery (and out of respect, more than anything else). They're paintings that scream and spit at you. And it's around this time that I learn about something called embodied cognition.

In terms of motor cell activity – the cells in the brain and spinal cord that enable us to move, speak, breathe and swallow by sending the commands to the right places – we can't actually tell the difference between doing something and seeing it done.[13] The neurological reaction behind this is known as embodied cognition. It's caused by our mirror neurons, which are the brain cells that behave in the same way both when an action is performed and when it's only observed. In other words, when *performing* an action, information flows out from the brain's control centres to the limbs; but in *observing* an action, the exact opposite happens to the same effect: information flows back into the control centres with the same message.[14]

Mirror neurons evolved primarily to help us better interact with and recognise the emotions of those around us. By reading body language – especially facial expressions – they allow us to automatically interpret the emotion behind them. Essentially, it's thanks to them that we connect to each other; they are the basis for empathy. Not just human either: we share them, in varying quantities, with all kinds of other life. From macaques to songbirds. And they fire up when we look at art, too, as even in static imagery mirror neurons turn what we see into emotion. Standing in front of an artwork you might feel a strange sense of knowing exactly how it was made (as if you were working on it yourself right at that moment). You could, in fact, be experiencing the exact same neurons firing as the artist did on making it, your brain forging new neural pathways as you look through the eyes of a maker. Perhaps you can feel the trajectory of the brushstrokes through your fingertips. The force it took to rip the canvas or melt the glue or burn the plastic (smell it). Every fine line and splatter. You are, at that moment, closer than looking. Experiencing as artist. Revel in it.

Like so many things, this was known long before we had the science to back it up. The Italian Renaissance Humanist Leon Battista Alberti wrote in his fifteenth-century treatise *On Painting*, 'We weep with the weeping, laugh with the laughing, and grieve with the grieving. These movements of the soul are made known by movements of the body.' A good painting cannot fail to move its audience – though perhaps only if they're willing to put a bit of time in. To return to the science briefly: the closer a work is analysed, the stronger the bidirectional flow and subsequently the viewer's experience of embodied cognition. In simpler terms: the harder the brain works at this, the more the viewer will be able to place themselves not just within the act of making, but in the specific scene depicted as well. I try this out in San Marco, the Florentine monastery complex decorated by the fifteenth-century monk Fra Angelico. Standing in one of the bare and tiny cells I study a frescoed crucifixion. I let the blood drip from my fingers, a tightness at each point nail has pierced flesh. It's a violence both quiet and jarring. It grabs me and brings me in; asking for nothing but my intense focus and giving everything in return. And what about the person who would have lived in the cell I was standing in, would have lived most of their life with this image for company? You can see how they were got.

As Alberti well knew, touch makes the abstract physical. And I think about the ways we bring the abstract into the body. I think of the wooden nubs of rosary beads, the feel of God on your very fingers. Human touch sure is a godly thing, transforming the most mundane into the spiritual. As an act, touch is rooted in all forms of spirituality; we clasp our hands during prayer, trace the sign of the cross on our bodies.[15] And even though I am not religious, I can't help but hold the flat press of a palm resting on the top of my head as something sacred. Touch connects us to ourselves, to others, and to the divine. This can be seen most evidently in religious ritual: activities that stretch right back into our evolutionary history. But what makes them so important – and what links them to touch? 'When you hold a particular belief you can feel pretty strongly about it,' says the neuroscientist Andrew Newberg, 'but if it is incorporated into a ritual, it makes it a far more powerful kind of experience, because it is something that you not only think about in your brain but feel in your body.'[16]

The world cannot simply be read. It is a space touched and a space embodied.[17] See, whatever happens or not to be inside of them, we are bodies after all; we can't truly understand anything without experiencing it. And because the world we live in can often be so abstract to us, sometimes we *have* to touch to be fully sure of it. Touch was considered by the classical philosophers as the most 'human' of all the senses: the only one we excelled at compared to all the other animals. For it was only touch, said the Roman writer Pliny, in which we ranked 'before all other species'.[18] We were made for the touching. Put down this book now and look at your hands. Although there are touch receptors all over the body, with an average of around two hundred in each square centimetre of the skin's surface, they appear most densely in the hands you have just held out to me. Each of ours contains about 17,000 touch-sensitive nerve fibres. Our fingertips are the most sensitive of all.[19]

'Unless I see the nail marks in his hands and put my finger where the nails were, and put my hand into his side,' the disciple

Thomas announces, on hearing of the resurrection of the crucified Christ, 'I will not believe.'[20] Look at him, in Caravaggio's *The Incredulity of Saint Thomas*: such dirty nails – you wouldn't have thought he'd dare do such a thing! But there he is in front of us, poking one of those filthy fingers right into the lance wound that Christ has pulled his robe open to show. Notice that the pressure caused by this action has stretched the skin around it almost into nothing. And how the wound wrinkles around the edges as Thomas pushes deeper. And notice, then, that Caravaggio has painted the wound as a mirror in minuscule to the disbelief drawn out all over the disciple's forehead. And that this shared physicality – of skin, that, though divine, behaves in such a human way – reminds us of the many other traits we share with these Biblical characters, and moreover, reminds us to stick at nurturing the rest of them. That Saint Thomas could climb right in, he's looking that closely.

Reality does seem to exist, I am realising, inside the body. Finding it is about winding the mind back and inside again and experiencing life in its actuality, rather than through theory or method. And mirror neurons help with this. They give us an intuitive sense of the world around us,[21] allow us to *know* before we *think*. During the seventeenth century, numerous European scholars and philosophers, including Descartes, tried to regulate feelings on the basis that they were untrustworthy, even dangerous. But though Descartes' glorification of rationality over emotion is still contributing to a mentality that exists today,[22] the rational does not hold much space for reality. And in alienating ourselves from our instincts, we become distanced not only from ourselves but also from everyone around us (however small and furry) who abide by theirs alone. Nietzsche wrote in 1882, 'I fear that the animals see the human being as a being like themselves who in a most dangerous manner has lost its animal common sense – as the insane animal, as the laughing animal, the weeping animal, the unhappy animal.'[23] It's that species loneliness again. Some of us are now so far from instinct we will have to listen hard, will have to tap into something that resides away from the mind and is sleeping far down in the darkness of those bodies of ours. (Hear the world hum with a forgotten resonance.)

Sometimes all it can take is a look. The feel of the night goes somewhere deeper. Outside the pub, pushed up against a car by your neck. Neither of you breaking each other's gaze.

One night I read a book called *Reality: A Very Short Introduction* and then can't sleep. What it lacks in size it makes up for in its sheer and existential power to make me feel worse. I should be pondering the nature of existence, but really all I want is a hug. That's touch again for you, bringing you right back inside the body. See, touch, in all its variety, has the power to shake us out of our heads and bring us into our physical selves – into these bodies of ours that exist on this earth right as you are reading these words. Touch brings us into the here and now, and this is what makes it pivotal in my search. It reminds me that reality really can be found in the most unexpected of places. I for one hadn't expected to find it bent over my kitchen table.

The smell of sap.
Wild horses the colour of peat.
The sun on heather, the whole rough lick of it.

V

Land

THERE WAS ONE SUMMER I became so desperate for sea and sky and solitude that I found myself a job on Iona, a minuscule island just off the west coast of Scotland. It only dawns on me now that it was actually reality I was after.

I'd always wondered how anyone could live somewhere like this. I pictured in my mind the sheer awesomeness of the land, and imagined the weather systems striking each inhabitant dumb each time they turned to the window of their thick-walled home. My daydreams showed me the islanders walking barefoot, their souls and hearts dug deep into the earth. They were made of soil and sand and the screech of gulls and brown peat water ran through their veins. I imagined that all islanders strode into their miniaturised landscape each evening, looked across to the surrounding small islands and the lapping waves and the seals and the dolphins and the basking sharks, and believed in some kind of holiness.

I must have been insufferable.

The cafe I am working in is run by three huge and intimidating sisters. They subtract the rent for my tiny bedroom from my paycheck. I buy my elderly vegetables from their overpriced general store, watching my small wage eat and regurgitate itself endlessly. Seven days a week, streams of Christian and pagan pilgrims flood the island, drawn either to the ley line that runs straight through it, or the early Christianity that was founded on its shores (or worse, both). One day I take payment for a bowl of chips and am met with 'Bless you and your family for seven generations' and then 'I can do that, you know'. A wry smile and off she goes while I am for that moment stupefied; the queue only getting longer and more agitated beyond the glass-fronted counter.

They are everywhere on the island, and they all have something to say to me. 'I can see you're not spiritual,' one of them tells me, an irritatingly attractive crystal-eyed pilgrim I meet walking to the beach across the island's golf course. This is not the first time I've been told this by a man. It's always men, and this damning insight invariably happens just before they come onto me, as if shagging spirituality into someone is how it's done (in which case I should be well on my way to enlightenment by now). Although this is not the first time I've been notified of my spiritual void, it has never been declared until now by someone who proclaims himself not one of the flock, but 'the Brother of Christ'. If this is true, I really have no hope. He has picked up a very loyal sheepdog on his travels. I look into its doleful eyes and think we must both have bad taste in men.

My insecurities lie lightly on my skin. Just a few months before this, a stranger in a textile shop in Bangalore had taken my hand and told me that he knew the reason for my desperation to escape into the hills, and would I like to know? Flustered, I declined and quickly left, blushingly ashamed of my emotional nudity.

Every day in the cafe I have to lie that our frozen prawns are freshly caught. I find it more offensive that I'm required to wear an overall. I am bullied by the chef and intimidated by the locals in the pub. One evening I knock a whole pile of live lobster out of the fridge, their chilled claws snapping in slow-motion as they skid across the kitchen floor and under the stainless-steel surfaces. I continuously misjudge the size of my cake slices and hide under the counter with the offcuts, frantically eating the evidence before I get caught. The internet is sporadic and I spend my evenings watching very slowly loaded films. They play out through my long working days in vivid intensity. Scorsese's *The Wolf of Wall Street* fills the place with New York bankers, all snorting cocaine off the counter and ramming sex workers up against my carefully curated biscuit selection. Loading *Amadeus* takes a week and I watch it in tiny segments, becoming so convinced I will be able to learn to read music without a piano that I try and teach myself, filling pages with notes like prose. Classical music plays constantly in my head. I am so lonely I think I am going insane.

Feeling groundless means you attach yourself to things in a slightly different way. It can be art, nature, architecture – anything that offers a visual timeline you can easily slot yourself into. And so, on Iona, lonely (and, because I am in my early twenties, emotionally and professionally lost) I find that it is only by immersing myself right into the physicality of the island that I feel like I exist at all. Between long and exhausting cafe shifts I slip off my shoes and walk. I take freezing dips in the clear sea. I write yawning reams of prose and overblown letters that nobody ever seems to answer, and take endless pictures of the views (all of which, on camera, look exactly the same). Every part of the island welcomes me. The grass is so interspersed with wild flowers, heather and moss that the whole surface is spongy, retaining indents of my footprints seconds after I've stepped away. Even the slugs are ode-worthy.

I leave at the end of the summer without having photographed one single person. I even censor myself out of my trip. It's as if, without visual evidence, I thought I'd be able to convince myself that it really had been all I'd hoped for; that it really was all just light, water and the soft-hilled land. Reading my diary years later, I found the words, 'I could not have imagined somewhere I would want to be more than Iona right now'. But I can't shake off the memory of how long the days were. Of how island light seemed to go on forever, how the silences were richer. I had forgotten the oddness of northern summer time, the way it became so supple and stretched I never quite believed it would end. But it was the land that kept me rooted to my decision; and something else, too, kept me company on those drawn-out and solitary days. I felt a presence on Iona so strongly there was no doubt in my mind the island was blessed.

Sometime before this, as a student in Glasgow, my housemates and I spent a summer visiting the petrified forest in Victoria Park. We'd lounge around on the grass beside the fossilised tree stumps, drinking bottles of cheap pink wine. The vicinity of these organic megaliths (325 million years old and counting, now available only in a dead-earth grey), made us feel that something significant was taking place on those long and placid afternoons. It's beautiful, I think, the steadfastness of something that will exist so much longer, and so much more assured, than we ever will. It's why I've often had the feeling that my reality might be hiding among the quiet gravitas of old trees; or infused, like spring warmth, in the weighted welcome of a standing stone. How better to root myself more deeply in my surroundings than to sit leant back against an object many thousands of years older than me.

Or to keep it closer still. For just a very short time, I had a perfect handprint on my body. Catching it in the mirror made me think of the clambering pattern of Argentina's *Cueva de las Manos*, of all those hands vying for attention for the last 13,000 years. The bruise had all but gone after a week; a fleeting antiquity on my skin.

Many of these ancient sites are now thought to have been used as physical portals through which individuals could enter the spiritual realm.[1] The imagery that remains on their walls – stencils, prints, finger painting – all evidence a visceral attempt at pushing through to the other side. *To get beyond the screen.* But they are also a record of touch, a reminder that far more holds us together than divides us. Here all of us are, all of us attempting to leave some kind of mark.

The artist Paul Nash called them 'personages': places and objects imbued with a particular charge – some feeling in the air around them that went far beyond their immediate physical impression. He found this in ancient sites; the atmosphere around standing stones often thick with it. Places where land and art meet.

Or, if not art exactly, then at least objects that have been put somewhere with purposeful intent. Strange groupings of trees, too. As a young man in 1911, Nash described south Oxfordshire's Wittenham Clumps as '. . . haunted by old gods long forgotten'.[2] Look at any painting, drawing or print of his, and you can't but see an ongoing attempt to decipher this language of our ancient lands.

I am in no doubt that the world outside has the power to piece me together when I am disparate and vague. I have intertwined my fingers into grass and felt more reality in one hand than in any other part of my body. But more often than not, though I yearn for it in the same abstract manner that I think so many of us do, the natural world gets me nowhere in my search. I do not share Nash's abilities in translation. This is no smooth dig, my spade often grates for days against rock. I write fast and badly and delete the whole lot of it. I go out and feel nothing. And it's moments like these that I am certain I'm speaking a different language to the world outside. Not to its residents, but to the trees, the grass, the hills and the waters. So often there is nothing out there for me.

Those early pandemic months of 2020, the late-afternoon sun-soft common next to my house kept appearing to me as two-dimensional as my computer screen. One afternoon out wandering I was nearly struck down by an elderly man cycling past, muttering 'bastard, bastard, bastard' under his breath. His rucksack and panniers were stuffed full of reduced-price Easter eggs. My skewed perspective of this strange and flattened landscape made it seem as if I had left my shadowed little study and walked straight out onto a piece of paper, onto the x-axis of a Cartesian plane. Tiny figures were scattered across the flatness: the furthest away in matte silhouette, the closer jogger or cyclist offering up a brief flash of themself before flitting away. It's very simple, existing in a drawing. Just one pencil line and a couple of tiny rectangles for houses. Maybe some scribbled trees. Nothing else. Nothing deeper than that, nothing more real than that.

Despite an inability to translate, we are today experiencing a resurgence of nature writing not seen with such momentum since the Industrial Revolution. Unlike the Industrial Revolution, though, our contemporary infatuation with nature is held together as much with images as it is with words. We are a population of image addicts, taking more photographs per minute than were made in the entirety of the nineteenth century.[3] And it's often nature towards which we turn the lens. Rather than a casual living-within, us urbanites make do with carving out slices of the natural world. We take them home and use them to soften the feel of our concrete days. Instagram has caged so many forests. So many autumn leaves held between so many anonymous fingers. Light, dappled, on so many surfaces. Nature today, you see, doesn't appear to exist until it is caught.

There is a particular time I remember, it had just snowed. And I walked in it and enjoyed it but what I failed to do was to take any pictures of it, and when I scrolled through everyone else's photos later the same day I started to doubt the validity of my own experiences. My own, like a jar with the lid half-unscrewed; and everybody else's captured and screwed tight and put on display, there to look back at and know for sure that a moment has been experienced. Because photographs tell us that reality has taken place, and will again. But what do we do with these jars? Just keep them there, stored, while the present escapes as ever at a fast trot?

(Somewhere out of reach, your reality exists healthy and well, living now only inside endless Facebook albums that also exist out of your reach, now you have deleted your account. There you exist, somewhere out there, untouchable.)

We're not the only ones who got used to looking at landscape through a screen. In the eighteenth century it became fashionable to literally turn one's back on it, and look instead at its reflection through the bulging oval of a 'landscape mirror'. These convex mirrors were made from darkened glass (glazed in any colour of your choosing), and offered a weak reflection of whatever landscape they were faced with. By reducing any vast panorama into a miniature and easily reproducible scale, the mirrors made the perfect tool for any artist. And as the bad-quality image would suppress most of the details, allowing only the most prominent features of the landscape to appear, the original view would be reinterpreted into something that already had a 'painterly' feel about it, making it easy for the artist to set down exactly what they saw on canvas. The mirrors became so popular that some of the wealthiest tourists would have large-scale ones specially made and fixed to the windows of their carriages, so that they could experience their entire journey as if sitting within a continuously changing roster of artworks by some of the best-established painters of their time (the same kind of immersive art experience that we are continuously sold today).[4] There you have it: the prototype of the Instagram filter. And over two centuries later here I am clicking into the app and doubting the validity of my own, unrecorded experiences.

See, ours for the most part is a culture of having. And any form of image capture is just another means to do this; photography an attempt, as Henri Cartier-Bresson tells us, 'to preserve life in the very act of living'.[5] It is a way to capture and hold onto our reality, a way to possess it – if such a thing were possible. But photographs only retain the past. And a semi-fictionalised one at that; innumerable narratives could be woven from the ones we choose to discard. Photographs fragment a life, turning the continuous cycle we all currently reside in into a series of moments, neatly packaged up for commemoration and display. 'All photographs are memento mori,' says Susan Sontag. 'To take a photograph is to participate in another person's (or thing's) mortality, vulnerability, mutability. Precisely by slicing out this moment and freezing it, all photographs testify to time's relentless melt.'[6] Present turns into past, and on and on. Things happening now captured as photos, neatly framed as memories, fading into half-remembered truths, nostalgia. But the present, how do we capture that?

The present is far harder to grasp than either past or future. Neurologically impossible, actually. Of that 10 million or so bits of visual stimuli hitting the retina every second (not to say all the other sensations hitting all the other parts of us), only around 600,000 can be transmitted through the optic nerve. About 1,000 of these bits arrive at the visual cortex, the small clump of brain that receives and processes anything coming in through the eyes. A unified world does consistently emerge from this mess, all of it integrated and processed into a singular presentation of the world outside,[7] but it's something as vague as the reflection of a landscape mirror. Out of this number (the 600,000) only a hundred or so from that original 10 million are used in our conscious perception – in other words, what we are seeing right in front of us.[8] And this action isn't immediate, so not only are we unaware of the most of it, we are actually always processing at a time-lag; once any of this information is cognitively available to us, it will already be in the past.[9] Which makes searching for the present the same as looking at a far-distant star. I've always known I was missing something, but seriously.

And with this in mind I wonder what if there were logic to our culture of image collecting? What if locking away these images is actually the only way that we humans have a chance at all in translating this lost and wild language? (A way of inching ever closer to a present that remains ever one step ahead of us?) What if Instagram, for all its failures, is actually working to encourage us to look closer? Each square on its grid a minute detail of a landscape, a shadow captured at play on the wall above our beds, the peculiarities of our faces studied in minutiae. Could the digital image really be today's means of translation, crucial to us all and achieved in the only way we are able? And is this the same for painting, how it condenses all those huge feelings and sights (and sites) into one. Through art, photography, writing, are we all just attempting to decipher an alphabet that no longer makes up our mother tongue? That perhaps never did?

Because it can be so dramatic, landscape, so dumbfoundingly beautiful that I just get stuck with what to do with it. Like my eyes aren't big enough or something. Or like I want to engage with it with more than I am. The feeling of it overwhelms me. Who even thought to make us so small up against all this vastness? Who even opened the door to these emotions, letting them right on into you without a real place to go? And with no space for them inside you, all that happens is you tear up; or maybe you swear to yourself or the person you are with. (I have to shout out of the car window whenever I drive through Snowdonia, it's that goddamn majestic.) Definitely you look and look, but it's never enough because you can't fill yourself up with it properly. And it's never there in the same way at all when you've turned away. And so it's got to be captured somehow, or you'll all be at a loss.

This brings me back to Nash, an artist who manages to draw us close into this mysterious language. His work is a balance between the seen and the unseen, each painting caught eternally between the recognisable and the surreal. Nash's landscapes seem to hold a secret they will only hint at – the same recognition we might experience while dreaming (comprehension scattered with every passing moment we are further from sleep). This is what makes the artist so compelling. His art stops us in our tracks and I, at least, cannot keep from looking; cannot keep from imagining walking down avenues lined by those lumpen trees, under skies that taste of peach Melba.

To really know where we are in all of this, we need something that demands us to stop. Because this is what it is to feel real. It is a being caught out, a falling out of rhythm with the moment-by-moment rush (exhausting and overwhelming and unconsidered). Paintings – they're moments preserved in such certain terms that even I cannot deny them. A sunset caught under cracked varnish, a wave in the split second before breaking (lined paper-thin, it is the ultimate wolf in sheep's clothing – an elegant disguise of such unhinged force). These are moments extracted, set down, contemplated and eternalised. Exceptional moments articulated within the everyday. Unlike us, paintings are inanimate objects. Or at least they move so slowly the changes are indecipherable until years later. Certain colours might have degraded into translucency, discoloured varnish transformed what would have been a summer landscape into the rich tarnish of autumn. But to all intents and purposes paintings are static, with little changing except our judgement on them. This is what makes art so continuously fascinating: this flow of opinion, gaze and theory over something that never changes what it's saying itself. Past, present and future all sharing the same ground. Paintings, to us in our whip-speed lives, are timeless.

I went to visit Nash's Wittenham Clumps on one of those slumpen-grey days that mark the beginning of a British new year. I wanted to see for myself what it was about that pair of wooded chalk hills that had triggered the artist's lifelong inspiration. But because I was already familiar with his work – been audience to his adaptations of these landmarks, rising dark and silent above the flat Oxfordshire fields – I could see them as only that. Painting and reality overlaid. Art seeping into life. What were in fact two ancient mud-dark and hibernating beech woods are painted in my memory with the soupy light of his *Landscape of the Vernal Equinox*.

It was us who did it, transformed the physical location into the subject; from *land* to *landscape*. Because it's a human creation, landscape: an intellectual home chiselled out from an uncaring, unyielding wild. When we animated the land with human concerns (with matters of the soul and psyche) we emptied it of farmers and manual labourers and filled it instead with nymphs, satyrs and woodland sprites. Deities vying for room alongside rabbit, deer and fox. A fictional and mythical glaze like a light frost over the whole lot of it. If we look back at Ancient Greek and Roman writing on the visual arts, we will discover fruit painted with such realism that garden birds were reported to have flown into the walls to peck at it; men falling into sticky and unsatiated lust with the chilled curves of marble sculpture; and the guard dogs for private homes petrified in stone, jaws open wide in their silent and teeth-bared bark.

Painting is a leg-up from the prosaic, and I would so rather a life witnessed in pinks and blues by those huge and weighted planets than to remember how things actually were (the blankness of winter, a flat view across sodden fields to Didcot power station).

I would so rather my surroundings translated. But untranslated, more often than not, has to do.

❧

A long time after my summer on Iona, I spend a year working in an often brilliant and always chaotic pub. As the manager, the chaos is usually my fault. I sleep for twelve hours on my days off and dream in real-time, twelve-hour shifts. Most mornings I wake up next to one of the barmen. I am never not at work, or rather, I keep accidentally bringing work home with me.

One morning the barman and I walk out. We continue walking for the next seven days, carrying only a hammock and a change of clothes, the whole hundred and twenty miles to the sea.

The journey takes us through an ever-changing English landscape. It is my favourite time of year to walk: everything late-August luscious – with all the trees so full of life they seem to be talking to one another, and the rivers lazy and generous. Henry David Thoreau once asked, 'What business have I in the woods if I am thinking of something out of the woods?'[10] Nature demanded Thoreau's full engagement. For him, to be somewhere physically but not in spirit was akin to not being there at all. Though without his knowledge, those same trees were releasing aerosols that were enabling him to relax, whether his conscious mind was on it or not. In 1854 Thoreau became so overcome with modernity he took to the forests of Massachusetts to live a simpler and more truthful life. To live, as he declared, '. . . deliberately, to front only the essential facts of life, and see if I could not learn what it had to teach, and not, when I came to die, discover that I had not lived'.[11] His reasons for escape beat a call to arms in me. And like Thoreau we too make our way through softly exhaling forests. Clouds of seed heads float across fields and we catch whole handfuls of them. Cultural immersion: that's supposed to be the best way to learn a language. I just hope – if I listen close enough to these wild places, if I tread enough of their ground, familiarise myself from the feet up – I'll somehow slip right in.

It is far from all idyllic though. A patchwork of forgotten trails we have linked together in our meandering route to the edge of England finds us tramping as much along the sides of A-roads thundering with lorries as in the midst of corn-shorn yellow-gold fields. Numerous times we are almost squashed as flat as the stinking badger carcasses we have to step around. We are always hungover, we are always hungry and we are always at least three hours away from breakfast.

On the first night I fall on my face out of the hammock and straight into a clump of stinging nettles. The next afternoon it rains so hard the water comes out of the top of my boots. We walk for hours across deep-furrowed fields, our feet dragging across the clay, wads of mud weighing us down. I'd had this romantic notion that this walk would turn me into Neil Ansell, who in the nineties spent five years living totally alone and self-sufficiently in the isolated hills of mid-Wales. He wrote afterwards of his experience not in terms of introspection, or of a deeper and more expansive self-awareness, but of just its opposite: a complete loss of self. Ansell achieved exactly what I was after – total immersion into the landscape. There was a winter before this walk that I'd wander along the river close to where I was living at the time; the wind blowing strange eddies in the water, tears streaming down my face, exposed skin burning with the cold, my nose running. And though all of me had wanted to be inside the experience, I'd felt completely constricted by my own body. My physicality stopping me enjoying this wild moment. I wanted to *be* it, only I was a tourist. Towards the end of his hermetic experience, Ansell wrote that he had all but disappeared from his own story; had become, as he described, 'a part of the landscape, a stone'.[12] Now that's true integration. Here's to sitting in the hills in silence that is soft and deafening. Here's to being those hills, that silence.

Even Thoreau struggled sometimes to achieve this feeling of assimilation though. 'I feel that with regard to Nature I live a sort of border life,' he once wrote, 'on the confines of a world into which I make occasional and transient forays only.'[13] Like Berger and his screen, Thoreau felt he had to surpass some immaterial substance to get right in. About a century later, the American Minimalist painter Agnes Martin expanded on this. 'Nature is like parting a curtain,' she said, 'you go into it.'[14] We want in. All of us.

In the midst of my impromptu journey, I realise that it's hard to completely lose yourself in nature when you're traipsing through a sodden field, mud spattering into your face with each step. I had never been more aware of my cold, uncomfortable physicality. And I was still not feeling real. And so looking back on this, from my own experiential evidence, it begins to appear to me as if complete awareness isn't the key to experiencing full reality after all. In moments like these, I realise, when you're so all-embracingly aware of your physical state, there's actually room for very little else, least not, as it turned out, reality.

Despite this, there remained things to be cheerful about. All this mud was actually working in its own way to nudge me a little closer into the present. *Mycobacterium vaccae*, a microbial bacteria that lives naturally in soil, acts as a natural antidepressant in humans.[15] Microbes have a serious impact on our physical and mental health. The more diverse *they are*, the less prone *we are* to inflammation in our bodies and brains. These microbes are known to be more diverse in rural areas, which is one of the reasons why cities are so bad for our health. The same goes for pollution. Our brains didn't evolve to absorb the toxic cocktail of chemicals spewed out by car engines and planes and factories and all else that keeps our cities running. (Cities are their own beast, working apart from and to the detriment of their human inhabitants.) Our brains react to this in just the same way they do to stress – by becoming inflamed.[16] And as we've already seen, stress has a serious effect on any of our ability to feel real. If nature actually does hold the key to reality, it's no wonder that chronic dissociation is a product of our time.

Along with it being a natural antidepressant, even just the smell of soil can be good for you. It stimulates the release of the hormone oxytocin: the same chemical that promotes bonding between mother and child, between lovers,[17] and the same chemical released when we look at art. So if my feelings of unreality are in part down to my mental health, then in the same way as looking at painting, being outside can only improve it. Regardless of this, right at that particular moment I was at a personal low. Though at least now I know that I probably wasn't depressed – only cold, wet and very, very miserable.

We walk for three straight days along the Ridgeway, the flint-strewn backbone of middle-England. Finally reach Wiltshire: a landscape where MOD tanks drive straight across ley lines, where the army hospital stands only a few hundred yards from Stonehenge. Here, just steps away from the ancient stones, we lay ourselves down, exhausted. Beside us a family is having a picnic. The granny sits silent in her wheelchair, which has been positioned facing directly away from the stones. I would like to have told her she wasn't missing much. It is the least spiritual place I have ever been to. Evocative of nothing. This could be down to the fact that Stonehenge is actually Welsh, a second-hand monument dismantled and dragged from Pembrokeshire to the Salisbury Plains around 5,000 years ago. Any of that presence (remember, the one that Nash was so aware of) must have been left behind, tramped into the mud of that hundred-and-forty-mile trudge. It's the Eiffel Tower in Las Vegas, the Louvre in Abu Dhabi.

Surrounding the regimented towns are warning signs and fenced fields, cut up and re-appropriated for target practice and scattered with mines. The chopped-up land taunts us as we walk through it. It is English countryside concentrate, quintessentially beautiful but totally unattainable. Everyone we meet is friendly to us because they assume we are in the army. We do nothing to tell them otherwise. An old general invites us into his garden for lemonade and regales us with in-jokes about regiments and we make out that we know what he's talking about. He pretends to squirt us with his hose and makes us try on a hat he bought in Egypt. We are very tired. He tells us about his army friends who will be visiting that afternoon and it's only later that we realise he was talking about an event that happened forty years ago.

In the pub we meet Gary. Gary is a warehouse robber cum animal rights activist who has built a beautiful allotment right next to the shooting range. He moved to this army stronghold because, as he says, 'it's the last place they'd ever look for me'. Gary offers us a bed for the night. We are full of cider, and optimism about our evening falling so easily into place (*this is the point of it all*, we think; *chance meetings, the kindness of strangers, this is surely the stuff of life!*). On the way to his, we stop in with one of his friends. The house smells of smoke and sadness, and even though it's a warm night none of the windows have been opened to let it out. We sit in the living room drinking Gary's friend's beers and smoking his roll-ups and he tells us about his tropical fish collection. A Channel 5 murder documentary plays in the background. I know the house cannot be his because there is a knitted loo roll holder in the bathroom, and he has placed a full ashtray on top of *Delia Smith's Complete Cookery Course*. And nobody familiar with Delia Smith would disrespect her in this way. Regardless, she smiles out at the desolate scene. I think she thinks he's a project.

Gary's wife will not let us in the house. One of their dogs is sick and she is holding an all-night vigil in the living room. Plus we are, as she says, complete strangers. We can only agree (it is unfortunate, but yes, we are complete strangers). Most of the fields are shooting ranges and we find so few options of where to string our hammock we resort to sleeping in a park. At four a.m. we are woken by the glare of a flashlight. Hearts pounding, we lie completely flat on the grass, faces hidden in our sleeping bags. We leave an hour later realising we have made camp in the middle of the front lawn of an enormous manor house. It takes us four hours to walk to the next town.

By the end of the journey the barman's boots are completely trashed. He limps the final ten miles in a pair of ancient flip-flops – the rubber divide popping out of each worn sole with every few steps. On the same day he goes deaf in one ear, my blisters get so bad I spend the morning walking on the sides of my feet. I get a mysterious rash all the way up my legs. The hammock strings break. But finally, we arrive. The destination of our pilgrimage, our very own Santiago de Compostela. Bournemouth.

We sit on a wall facing away from the sea, heads in our hands.

Bournemouth is overcrowded and full of chain pubs. We see a pug in a pram, with a baby-pink fan attached to it blowing air straight into the unblinking water of its eyes. We see an elderly woman on a mobility scooter blasting dance music. We can't afford to buy the chips. We stand with our feet in the sea and wonder why we came here. But somehow, *somehow*, through the exhaustion, the rain, the miles of verge and mud, the bites stings scratches and relentless monotony, the very act of walking has done its trick.

It's easy to be somewhere and not be there – maybe because you're tired, or bored, or anxious, or thinking about the future. And because you're not feeling there, you will undoubtedly want to be somewhere else, somewhere you are sure will give you a feeling of 'there-ness'. It doesn't work like this. Place, I've realised, doesn't have the power alone to grant this feeling. Because when you are somewhere and *there* – and I mean *mind–body there*; I mean pure, in-the-moment feeling of reality *there* – your surroundings may actually be completely irrelevant. The moment becomes more important than the place. When your mind and body are just so, it doesn't matter where you are. You know full well that in that particular moment you can say, and this with one hundred per cent certainty, you are *here*. It is a fine and beautiful balance, but it exists. And right at that point in time, there I was in myself. Bournemouth beside the point. We vow never to return, but the feeling, I was and still am certain, will.

One of Thoreau's derivations of the word saunter is *sans terre*, literally *without land*. He translates this as 'having no particular home, but equally at home everywhere'.[18] Moving through a space I sometimes struggle to quite believe in, can help to clarify its existence to me. The miles walked had somehow reiterated us back into ourselves. Inside our broken bodies, we were at home. It is only much later that I discover the word ecology was derived from the Greek 'oikos', for home. Once again, this is what it comes back to.

VI

Water

THEN THERE'S WATER. Water in all its thirst-quenching heart-stopping deep-velvet summer-night skin-slip-naked dip-ping glory.

I am standing in the tide of the most beautiful beach I have ever been to, and I am thinking about fractals. The beach, on this outlandishly warm early autumn day, could be anywhere in the world, but instead it is in west Wales. The white-gold light makes a reflective surface of almost the entire landscape. Huge cliffs are slatted diagonal and deep right down into the wet sand, and the vastness and the brightness of the whole lot of it makes me squint. Nothing but the bite of the fresh salt air. (I want a dress made from the exact deep purple of the sea anemone. Nails the colour of seaweed.)

Earlier that day, the barman and I had walked along cliff tops above the misted sea. Tiny flowers in the grasses were dried crisp right where they had grown in the soft-sprung soil; the blackberries huge and salted. We are in that strange and sad no man's land that comes just before the end of a relationship: where everything is exactly as it ever was, but nothing feels quite right. As we walk, apart and in the quiet, we watch the shining black choughs perform disappearing acts as they dive-bomb straight-vertical into the gullies. The mist makes me wonder, not for the first time, if I might be dead. Regardless, I'm in fairly good spirits. There's something I find oddly satisfying about being melodramatic beside the ocean. There is nothing quite so sad as the British seaside; the sheer run-down forced fun of it lending itself as generously to family holidays as it does to despair (often in the same afternoon). The cliffs are right next to a military base and the woodpecker I am excited to be hearing turns out to be distant machine-gun fire.

That same afternoon we'd been sitting on the steps of a monument in the centre of a small seaside town. Below us an elderly man in an electric wheelchair was on his iPad, intently scrolling through a webpage of women's underwear. From our perch we'd seen a father so exhausted by his cycling holiday with his desperately enthusiastic wife and highly athletic adult children that he rode up the road away from them and pretended to scan a cafe menu, determinedly, for almost twenty minutes. In the town everyone had a small dog and all these small dogs kept yapping at each other. Lots of the tourists were cold in their summer clothes and some of them had ice creams but looked as if they wanted to cry. The evening before this, flares had held themselves bright orange in the sky over our campsite as we cooked our pasta.

But right now I am standing in the gleaming tide of the most beautiful beach I have ever been to, and I am thinking about fractals. As I stand here, the sand weighted beneath my feet, I feel the water come to me, pull away, come to me. Again.

A fractal, in its most simple of terms, is a never-ending and self-similar pattern; a rough or somehow fragmented geometric shape that repeats itself exactly across an entirety of different scales.[1] If I were to pan up and outwards, looking from above at this ancient and dramatic Welsh coastline, I might find that, along with the movement of the ocean and the weather-blasted trees, the swept and cragged shore contains these self-similar fractal patterns too. There is a reason that, as Benoit Mandelbrot, the Polish mathematician who coined the term fractal in 1975, put it, 'Clouds are not spheres, mountains are not cones, coastlines are not circles, and bark is not smooth, nor does lightning travel in a straight line'.[2] Fractal coastlines, with their large surface areas, are able to absorb the energy of the hurling waves far better than any non-fractal shape ever would. And when a coastline is *less* fractal, the waves go to work on it, breaking down the rock until it becomes more so. This symbiotic relationship between water and land is a self-stabilising system that keeps us on dry ground. Just like this coastline, each one of us, too, is formed by the forces that impose themselves on us, both violent and subtle (over and over and over again). My own formation took nothing more than a blink compared to the repetitive bite of this small island, ground into shape by the continuous crashing of the waves, the daily rise and fall of the water, the shift of tectonic plates.[3] So many thousands of years of going through the same motions. Water is remarkably patient. I am not. But still it is here – right where I am in this slow landscape, in this ankle-lick of sea – that reality comes calling for me. I gaze out at the incoming tide. Without warning, I find myself simultaneously relaxed and focused; utterly, as if the light and the water and the repeating and repeating shapes are all I am. The tide washes in and away, unfailingly. No worries, no distraction. All else eliminated. And so it happens again. I feel real.

What is it? Does the relative languor of the water offer me some kind of respite from my flickering, digitised brain? Or could it be the sound instead? Cognitive neuroscientist Petr Janata theorises that the sound of water, the low frequency of it coupled with its rhythmic nature, matches the frequency and rhythm of human breath. But Shelley Batts, Senior Research Fellow at Harvard Medical School, takes us far further back, linking the sound to the amniotic intimacy inside the womb.[4]

In the 1980s, environmental psychologist couple Rachel and Stephen Kaplan posited the importance of something they termed Attention Restoration Theory. Directing too much attention on a single thing, they argued, led to mental fatigue. The cure? The effortless attention instigated by immersion into a natural landscape. The Kaplans called this 'soft fascination': the uncomplicated and involuntary occupation of the mind when all senses are engaged with nature.[5] And it is a scientific fact that water in all its capacities has the ability to calm both body and mind.[6] Whatever its methods, even just the sound of water can bring us back to ourselves. And then there's the air all about it. Crashing waves, waterfalls, fast-moving rapids – anywhere air molecules are broken apart by moving water, negative ions are released into our surroundings. Ingesting these negative ions has been linked to the release of that all-important feel-good chemical, serotonin. Not just linked to happiness, serotonin has a positive effect on memory and our ability to learn. It regulates digestion and body temperature, improves sleep quality and can enhance sexual desire. Lack of serotonin in the body plays a part in a number of health conditions, including depression, anxiety and mania.[7] Positive ions do the opposite. Released in winds like the mistral, sirocco and chinook, they send people disoriented, depressed and often physically unwell. Ill winds, undoubtedly.

It may be in the air, but the feeling of reality that water can provide is also down to fractals. Research carried out by the University of Oregon professor Dr Richard Taylor, in the early 2000s, found a direct correlation between observing fractals and stress. His results suggested that, when viewing a broad range of different types of fractals (including snowflakes and the work of the American Abstract Expressionist Jackson Pollock), research participants experienced a reduction in stress levels, reaching instead a focused yet completely relaxed state.[8] This description is so similar to what I have found reality to be comprised of, it would be illogical of me to ignore it; and when I look at these same results, I conclude that fractals also cause an increase in reality. Because the feeling that I'm talking about isn't one in which I'm totally spaced-out or slightly high. Far from it. It is an inherently grounded presence, a moment in which I have the absolute certainty of being nowhere else.

Fractals are found throughout the natural world; they are in the patterns of our water systems and our mountain ranges. They exist in something as minuscule as the membrane of a cell and in the emptied vastness of the solar system.[9] Head into the forest and you'll find fractals with every step: from the satisfaction of the pinecones scattered on the forest floor to the fern leaves, lush and shaded. Raise your head and there above you you'll see fractal shapes in the branches of every tree. And if then, you crouch, dig a hand right down into the soil, you might find your fingers tracing the fractal patterning of fungal mycelium, communicating there in the darkness. But why do fractals have this effect on us? Is it that they lock us in? Set us within the wider context; the world as an interlocking whole in which we play our vital part?[10] Here we stand locked into the universe, which continues to lock into itself.

And in the same way that over half of our bodies are made up of water, the same way that eighty percent of our brain is made up of it (water on the mind, quite literally),[11] *we* consist of fractals too. Open yourself up and take a close look at your lungs, veins and eyes; you'll discover all kinds of fractal elements. And so however complex the fractals that exist outside of our own bodies are, we have what Taylor describes as a physiological resonance.[12] No deciphering is needed – looking at a fractal is nothing but the right key in the right lock. I find it reassuring to know that however cluttered our minds are, our brain is a fractal too. These patterns can do nothing else but directly bind us to our home planet, however distantly we have strayed.

The writer John Briggs called fractals 'the patterns of chaos'. Because believe it or not, chaos has a pattern too. And chaos – that confused, shape-shifting nonentity – has long been associated with water;[13] a tempestuous mishmash of primordial sea in which everything is mixed up, and from which all life was born. For the Roman poet Ovid, right at the beginning

'... the countenance
Of nature was the same, all one, well named
Chaos, a raw and undivided mass,
Naught but a lifeless bulk, with warring seeds
Off ill-joined elements compressed together.'[14]

The same goes according to the Book of Genesis: 'And the earth was without form, and void; and darkness was upon the face of the deep. And the spirit of God moved upon the face of the waters.'[15] Dredge the dark and directionless depths of chaos and you will discover the origin stories of ancient Egypt, Babylon; of Hawaii and Native America. Look up, if you can make out which direction it is, and you will see the thick and wetted mists of Chinese mythology.[16] Before all else, there was water. Water as chaos, chaos as fractal, fractal making sense of even the most elaborately complex. Dürer knew this, once saying to a friend of his, the German theologian Philip Melanchthon, 'When I was young, I craved variety and novelty. Now, in my old age, I have begun to see the native countenance of nature and come to understand that this simplicity is the ultimate goal of art.'[17] Once again, it all comes back to simplicity.

Fractals are found in art too. To avoid the figurative image, the fractal is used in the sacred patterning that depicts the divine in Islamic art and architecture. It makes me wonder if the ease with which one can get lost in those interlocking golden knots is comparative to prayer – pattern as a means for us to more easily comprehend the eternal. And then if that same divinity can be sought by gazing at the ocean. The two are undoubtedly linked. (The prophet Jeremiah twice describes God as 'the spring of living water'.)[18]

In the late fifteenth century, the artist Sandro Botticelli illustrated a manuscript of Dante's *Divine Comedy*. As Dante and his celestial guide Virgil travel away from the teeming and beastly depths of the Inferno, both his language and Botticelli's illustrations become increasingly abstracted. Once they have made their way to the very peak of Paradise, they find themselves outside of time and space, in a heaven 'which is pure light alone'.[19] Most of the artist's drawings this far into Dante's journey contain almost nothing but the pair surrounded by flaming stars, empty space and concentric circles. I was stopped stunned when I first saw these illustrations, to think that the artist behind *Primavera* and *The Birth of Venus* – works of such elaborate and rich decoration – could strip down his practice in such a way. Each holds so much more reality than any aged hand emerging from a cloud, more than skies filled with puppy-fatted putti (all those tiny wings beating just the smallest of breezes inside the frame). I think of the sublime little party later unstrapping them, those wings. Lines where the leather has cut into soft white skin – shoulders tender from so many hours of wear. The small actors head to the bar after the final encore. Leaving gilt frames filled with cloud, ethereal light, not much else. It's that space that does it. I am certain that there was more of the divine in Botticelli's emptied pages than I'd found in any of the old churches I've ever been to.

Anyway, I'm meandering. Like a river.

While Herman Melville's Ishmael turns to the sea '. . . whenever it is a damp, drizzly November . . .'[20] in his soul, I look inland, to the rivers. River swimming has been my most longstanding cure for reality loss. It is an all-season method, and well-shared too; one in which I have been as prone to leap in on a summer's wander as to emerge, mottled skin and bluing lips, in the depths of winter. I like the smell of it and the slip of the pebbles. I like the cuts and scratches that only make themselves known to me as I thaw: the love-bitten markers of my brief and transformative immersion left by whatever roots or brambles or powdery bank I have had to slide down in order to get in. I like scrambling out and putting clothes back on over a dampened body covered in leaf and weed and rubbed with earth, a body dirtier yet somehow far cleaner than it was pre-immersion. I use cold water in the way that so many of us do: to shift the mugginess in my head, to feel chilled right to the edges of my body at the times when I'm not sure just where the edges are. I use it to sharpen my awareness and for that shock-hit of adrenaline that convinces me that there is nothing else in existence but the present.

There are an estimated 42,700 miles of stream and river that criss-cross the United Kingdom like loose knitting. You might assume from this that there would be enough room for us all, but only 1,400 of those miles have right of public access (that's just three percent).[21] The issue here, though, is more than one of access. Our rivers are not only being taken away from us, with water companies openly pouring untreated sewage into them on a daily basis, they are being soiled. On writing, less than one-fifth of English rivers are healthy and they continue to degrade. We still swim, loads of us, but now with our heads above the water rather than below it, which feels far too formal for the freedom both we and the rivers know they can inspire in us.

But water doesn't always hand reality to me in this quasi-Arcadian manner. It is not always glowing, golden-hour beautiful

and can be something far more powerful than the late-summer gentleness or the deeply sleeping winters of the British countryside. There are times I've been reminded in just one instant of the sheer size of it all, of the comparative insignificance of our own and tiny domain. I found myself, once, a natural bathtub carved out of volcanic rock, immersed into the floor of a wide-mouthed cave right on the roaring edge of the Atlantic. It was a black and roughened landscape. The rock like gurning faces: petrified in the exact place the lava had first reared and sputtered into life. The pool was filled a clear blue and right at its base sat a bed of small pebbles, each one almost the perfect circle. And all around – everywhere except for this still, enchanted place – the ocean hurled itself. I stole one (one stubbled shriek of a face), dropped it into my bag and then took off my clothes and
slipped right in
to the generous
dip.

But the land – it wanted me out. One enormous wave, from which I was only saved because there were hands that grabbed at me the moment before the water pulled back. Scraped me into safety and away from those faces that I swear had been screaming.

It was reality though. A brutal kick of it, manifested as pure fear. There are few instances in day-to-day life where one feels on such a knife edge between safety and disaster, and for a long time afterwards I felt more as if I'd been tossed across the lava and swept out far into the ocean than at all in my own body. My experience (or more to the point, the almostness of it) left me curious about what might so easily have happened. If only, like a parent flipping a child's nightmare on its head, I could clamber through that fear, then I'd be able to see what exists on the other side, see if *I* could too. Later there was another beach (with black sand that *glittered*) where we walked barefoot along a shore, with the tide's pull so strong that, when we looked back at the distance we'd covered, we realised we'd veered right into the water.

By the time we returned to the UK my lump of lava had lost its face and its voice, and it is now nothing but an inanimate alien sitting quietly on a kitchen shelf.

In the last years of the fifteenth century, fear of an upcoming apocalypse took an extraordinary hold on the western mind. The end of centuries (and of course, as many of us have experienced in our own lifetimes, the beginning of new millennia) have always been associated with a rampant paranoia about the destruction of the known world. This was intensified in the fifteenth century by the invention of the printing press. Panic-inducing prophetic writings spread across the whole of western Europe, coupled with thousands of cheaply produced images illustrating the upcoming catastrophe – brilliant and monstrous scenes of the final fight between good and evil, the war to end all wars. Attempts were made by the church to temper the hype, but still many people made preparations. Homes were boarded up or sold, their former inhabitants fleeing to the hills; in Germany whole villages lay deserted.[22] It was as senseless as all mass panics are, but it took up space in even the greatest and most deeply empirical of minds.

Leonardo da Vinci's *Deluge* drawings, made between 1517 and 1518, depict cataclysmic waters crashing over minuscule villages, snapping tree trunks and crushing houses in instantaneous destruction. Each drawing is smaller than an A4 sheet of paper. Each drawing terrifies me.

I visit them at their home in Windsor Castle on my way to catch a flight to Sicily, where I will be spending a month working and writing. My suitcase drags heavy over the royal cobbles; as an avid anti-monarchist I blame the Crown for the fact the wheels no longer seem to be working. It has taken me two years to successfully organise a visit to these drawings and I have inadvertently arrived on the eve of the Platinum Jubilee. Everything is covered in Union Jack bunting and there are terrible royal portraits in the windows of soulless commercial galleries. I have never seen so many people eating scones. It makes me want to kick something over, but instead I give the Royal security all of my personal details and get escorted into the print room.

Leonardo was fascinated by virtually everything he saw. But for all of his interests, the most continuous, the most obsessive, was with the movement of water. There is something in the quantity and quality of the artist's works and research themed around this subject that marks it somehow different from anything of either a strictly practical or theoretical interest.[23] His drawings bear the marks of a compulsion that seems as intimate as it is one of pure desperation; the same dedication devoted to each liquid curl as to those on the golden heads of any of his angels. Graphite moves as liquid through his hands.

Although there are descriptions of similar disastrous events in his notebooks, the deluge drawings are without the explanatory texts that usually accompany Leonardo's studies. They neither represent the Christian interpretation of the end of the world, which comes not by water but by fire, nor are they representations of the Biblical flood.[24] This makes them somehow worse. They speak of a nightmarish and illogical fear outside of either religion or rationality. And how could Leonardo have studied the sensitive mechanics of the body for so many years and not compared his own human frailty to the awesome force of nature? He must have had full knowledge that, if it came to it, his stolid *Vitruvian Man* would be obliterated in less than a heartbeat (imagine him rolling, his spherical home thrown about by those tumultuous waves).

Hard to comprehend the magnitude of the disaster depicted until you notice the minute houses, church turrets, tiny villages surrounded by abandoned fields. A dwarfing of everything we might once have thought grand (the inconsequence of it all). People too small here to be included, but surely there as well, in mind if not in sight. And I do keep seeing faces: one with a leering grin right at its epicentre, and in another I find the head of a deer, or a hare perhaps – eyes alert and staring straight out and into my own. But the best thing of the whole lot of them is just one tree, bent almost double under tearing winds. A sheen of water is pressed hard against each leaf (each drawn individually, minuscule, imagine!). Feel the frigid windswept state of it, just by looking.

Each of Leonardo's deluge drawings feels on the brink of exploding out of the paper and charging right over its audience. It's funny, because when I look back at the photos I took while I was there, I find reflections of my hands (white-gloved, of course) in each, as if we were one and the same. As if the disaster had already happened and I was just another body in the mix. And a mix not just made up of water either. Leonardo's deluges are tumbling paroxysms of air, cloud and rain, engulfing everything in their path. In a word, they are chaos.[25] But, just like chaos, look closer and you will discover that these drawings abide by the laws of nature. The movement of water in each work holds true to the science; each wave affecting its neighbour, its neighbour, and so on.[26] The obsessive accuracy in Leonardo's deluge drawings makes me see them not just as priceless works of art, but as a visual record of an individual attempting to understand, or even to rationalise, the thing that scares them most; commanding something they have no actual ability to control. And control, I guess, is something I'm after. A mastery of my own reality, in whatever shape it might take.

Just over a decade later, in Germany in 1525, our friend Albrecht Dürer documents a similar fear. He has a dream that shakes him deeply: of enormous plumes of water tumbling straight down from the heavens and thundering onto the ground. 'I was so frightened when I awoke,' he writes, in a long and vivid description of the dream included just below the watercolour he goes on to make, 'that my whole body trembled and for a long while I could not come to myself.' The fear has dislodged him. And it's art he uses in his attempts to understand it, art that brings him back to himself. The small watercolour is still in existence, five hundred years after the artist woke up the morning following his dream and rushed from his bed to paint it. It could be a Paul Nash, it feels that modern. And with the same candy-coloured surrealness; golden fields in front of what brings to mind a nuclear explosion, depicted in a fetching cornflower blue. Dürer has managed to transform this nightmarish fear into something of such simplicity, such clarity, that the more I study it the more I find myself inexplicably close to tears. There's something inherently intimate about a watercolour. Quick-drying, every mark made remains on the paper. (Even part-obliterated, a ghost will linger.) Looking at Dürer's, we are able to track every movement of the artist's hand as he transformed his mental image into something of substance.

Transformation comes in many forms, and it has a long-established relationship with water. Look to the skies right now and you may be lucky enough to see the clouds making this apparent. Perhaps you will see a scud of waves above you, or that weighted cover a moment before the rain. Water has cooled and eternalised rivers of burning lava into strange and mythologised shapes; it is at the beginning of all of our stories but drips and slows and stops too, ending them as stalactites that hang silent in dark and undiscovered caves. It can shift over the earth's surface with ease, disrupting and destroying everything we have perceived to hold firm.

It's no wonder, then, when we see water transform states daily, that our ancient belief systems gifted it this power in ways less abiding to the laws of nature. For the ancient Egyptians, the first humans were transformed out of the sweat and tears of the sun god, Ra. And in our more recent Classical past, Prometheus (known as the god of trickery) mixed water with earth and shaped mankind from the muddy heap (making you wonder how much of this decision to create us was a practical joke).

Water's slippery way also lent itself perfectly to the love games and revenge of the gods. They were always transforming each other, back then; and, depending on whose fingers it had poured through, water could be a dangerous tool. So knew the young hunter Actaeon. When he caught the virgin goddess Diana bathing with her nymphs, she weaponised the only thing she had to hand

> *'. . . and flung it in the young man's face*
> *And as the avenging downpour drenched his hair*
>
> *She added words that warned of doom: 'Now tell*
> *You saw me here naked without my clothes,*
> *If you can tell at all!'*[27]

With this watery curse Actaeon is transformed into a stag; to be torn apart by his own dogs, who of course no longer recognise him as their master. But water is not just used for revenge, it is a tool for salvation, too; its use in this way evident when the sea nymph Galatea turns her beloved Acis into a river, after he is crushed by the jealous and brutish cyclops, Polyphemus. Water is also quite the addition to any mythological recipe. Aphrodite, goddess of love, was created from seafoam mixed with the blood of the castrated Cronus. The antique landscape teems with ethereal life. A walker in its midst must be cautious. A swimmer, even more so. You may well climb out not just chilled to the bone but a completely different species.

Water enables spiritual transformation too. Christenings, baptisms, full-body immersions into the filthy waters of the Ganges; it is the chosen medium of the divine, world-over. And it gets right into the subconscious, as well. For the twentieth-century Swiss psychoanalyst Carl Jung, water even *is* the subconscious – that formless, unbound state. And, just like the subconscious, water hides and reveals
hides and reveals
hides and reveals

We remain fascinated by the lost city of Atlantis, but have all but forgotten the flooded community of Capel Celyn. Water, like us, is often contrary.

But let's step back into the body, momentarily (and in whatever shape it now holds), because water certainly took a prime role in transforming us. Our earliest-known ancestor is thought to be a microscopic sea-dwelling species named *Saccorhytus*. It lived 540 million years ago, was shaped like a plastic bag, and had only a very large mouth and no anus. It measured one millimetre in size. Not recognisable features for the most of us, but one trait in our shared lineage does remain: our very human connection to the bodies of water that make up so much of our home planet.

In Ischia, an island just off Naples, there are hot springs that bubble up from the seashore. There is a man there who lives in a cave all summer and sells hard-boiled eggs he cooks at points where the sea is rolling with heat. 'Uovo! Uovo!' he shouts. 'Egg! Egg!'. From the very top of the hill and looking down, you'll see the warm little pools are lumped and full with bare and fleshy tourists. And from this viewpoint, where the great undressed look like nothing more than gatherings of miscoloured tadpoles residing in a warm mulch, it is hard to believe that much evolution has happened at all. Later, when I go into the warm volcanic waters myself, I feel briefly what I can only describe as an evolutionary peace. Those were simpler times. I can't say it gives me any striking feeling of reality though. Unfortunately, I am soon distracted by a loud American eating a sandwich in his swimming trunks. Scattered crumbs float past me in the wash and once again all I can think about is being somewhere else.

I am, however, more than willing to immerse myself in this long-held understanding of water as a transformative power if it will get me closer to my objective. And so soon after my return from the Welsh coast, I take myself to a holy well. Holy wells are one of those pockets of confusion that you can find so often in the British countryside. Places where superstition is bound to religion is bound to local tradition. Places where the boundaries of all are hazy. I go on an afternoon where reality isn't too much of an issue. Bright sunny days can do this. Days that are so there and in-your-face and glorious that the feeling I often have of my life as a memory just doesn't matter, because even the memory is so brilliant and fresh and pure. The sun shines with a chilled warmth that hints at autumn; the nettles reaching out of the bracken and stinging me repeatedly. I rip my tights climbing over fences. Above me, huge white clouds move over the miles of green-fielded hills. And the wind is the thing that touches it all. Later, I walk through an oak wood bedded with dried leaves. The breeze down among the trees is loud, and shadow and light play fast and chaotic on the forest floor. Acorns and leaves and twigs drop into my hair; I feel like a child among the legs of drunk and gesticulating adults.

I do not find the well. What I do find, though, is a stone sheep trough filled with such disconcertingly clear water I wonder for a moment if I should just make do. It turns out that the well is actually in the grounds of a thickset and whitewashed church just around the corner from me. I have been scrabbling up the rutted slopes in completely the wrong direction. In essence, this seems to sum up my entire problem.

The house just below the church has huge plastic dinosaurs in its garden, as if in protest to living in the ecclesiastical shadow. Regardless of the truth in our reptilian forefathers though, I decide to put myself in the hands of the water – be it pagan, Christian, or, as it turns out, just slightly stagnant. An elderly couple sitting on a bench in the church car park watch me as I stride past, clutching my notebook and pen under my arm, ever prepared to document all the feelings I do and do not have (yes, I am beginning to feel faintly ridiculous). The church is cast completely in shadow, and now that I've finally arrived the whole experience takes on a slightly furtive air, as if by creeping around the side of it I'm doing something I shouldn't. The well has a DANGER sign attached to it (though I imagine due to the few wet slate steps that lead down to the square of dark and leaf-sludged water, rather than the possibility of dramatic religious conversion). I think to myself that I might actually have preferred the sheep trough. I hadn't quite planned what I'd do when I arrived. Drink it? Baptise myself? Rub it on my eyelids? Instead I splash my face with it, three times. Because washing your face is always the right decision, and I have in my head that the number three has some kind of magical connotation about it.

And then I sit on a bench and wait for something to happen. It sounds stupid, and I guess it is. But it's the kind of thing I've resorted to: tramping the countryside to find some kind of cure for a problem that I can barely describe in ways that will make sense to anyone else. And anyhow, it's less stupid than the alternative. What I really don't understand is how, through my unscientific research journey, *I* am the one who is doing something unusual, when all I am trying to do is to spend my time on this planet in a way that has some kind of depth to it. To me it seems to be the most logical thing of all. I'm so bored of repeatedly hitting the barrier between me and the rest of the world, when all I'm doing is just attempting to walk on through.

Of course all that does happen is that my face dries slowly in the sun. I look at the trees and everything is quiet. The water in my eyelashes makes the landscape shine, but that is it. I think of how people who swim in rivers, in just the same way, in fact, as people who partake in BDSM, often talk of an abstract spirituality, a feeling of oneness. And this makes sense – it's easy to be spiritual in water, since it has lent itself to spirituality, really, since we began to lend ourselves to the divine. I think of our bodies, too; how we are composed of the exact same atoms that make up the world around us, how each one of our cells is enclosed in a membrane that needs water for its structure and function – meaning every living organism perceives the world through the substance.[28] (I imagine swimming with leaking goggles, and condensation on the inside of windows.) It's easy to forget, when on dry land, how far from solid we actually are; how we exchange molecules with every breath we take, every bite we eat. The human body has a similar density to water, and so once immersed we become all a mix, able to merge the bits that have come apart. In water, a space without hard edges or sharp corners (a place without hard thoughts or sharp words), the flow of the physical becomes more easily apparent.

And like water, we are also linked to the pull of the moon. What with the brain being part liquid, the ancient Greeks and Romans would have us believe, we could be affected by it in just the same way as the tides. Since antiquity it's been blamed for all kinds of mischief caused on our own planet; lunacy, for the ancients, ebbed and flowed. As do we. Viewed all together, and from a far distance, we might appear as flowing waterways; all of us under just the same cyclical influence as the tides. And us women, cyclical too (Diana, crescent moon braided right into her hair, our rightful goddess). The moon's pull on us is lessening though. It moves away from us incrementally, at about the same rate as our fingernails grow.

The science writer Loren Eiseley once described humans as '. . . a way that water has of going about, beyond the reach of rivers'.[29] There's something in this that I can't get out of my mind; bound by water, a vessel for its whims. It's no wonder we've retained its emotional pull – water is a part of our deep evolutionary past. Is part of reality somehow getting our bodies back to these origins, I wonder? However long-distant they may be. Maybe this is all it is. Cold water, nothing more nothing less, maybe that's all that's required.

Sometimes I make myself concentrate on the actual feel of it. Just the slice of it across my finger puts the whole lot of me back in my place.

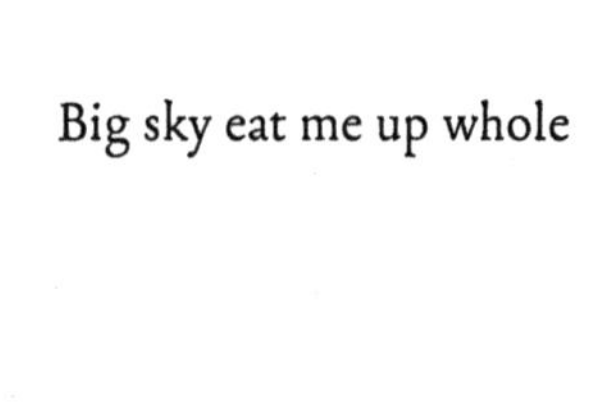
Big sky eat me up whole

VII

Sky

It's the summer of 2020 and I am living in Cambridge in a tiny bedroom I share with the barman and our mutual unhappiness. The house is filled with the unmourned-for remains of past occupants; empty spirit bottles, wine-spattered guitar amps and old and lumpen cushions that cover the stained sofas. We are broke and friendless and have only one bike between us, taking it in turns to ride to work.

On the weekends, the barman and I go on aimless walks around the surrounding villages. In one, we find a sign on someone's fence that says, 'DOG SHIT. I have CCTV. I know who U R. Do it again and the whole village will too'. Another time we ricochet down onto a disused train track (discarded clothing, a solo trainer, dirty plastic bags you'd be well advised not to look into). The air has a chill about it, as if we have inadvertently slipped underwater, but when we emerge out onto the other side we are in a huge ploughed field, everything warm and golden as if we have stepped onto somebody else's colour palette. Later that same evening, when I say to the barman we should start planning our future, he replies, 'What future?' and so instead we plan another walk. He lies on the bed, fully clothed and in silence with the map of Cambridgeshire over his face. Downstairs in our kitchen there is an ancient and sporadically vomiting cat called Jimmy. Its fur begins to fall out in clumps and often I find it sitting in the middle of the floor staring out at nothing. A lot of the time I feel like I'm floating.

Sometimes the barman and I drive out onto the flat lick of countryside that surrounds the city and stay overnight bundled up in the back of the car. One evening there is a sunset that turns all the cornfields pink; the final remaining sliver lasting well into the night. We'd fallen out, and watch it in silence sitting on a gate on the edge of a busy A-road, swigging out of a bottle of red wine. Cars scream past us. I wake up freezing and see the brightest stars out of the window. All the sounds of the night, and the sea in the far distance – noise carrying for miles over those strange and unbroken levels. Carrying for miles under the enormity of those skies.

We weren't going anywhere special, the first time we discovered them. Just driving aimlessly about as we were wont to do back then. When, out of nowhere, clouds panned in from all directions: miles of them low over the golden flat, so huge one might assume it was their weight that had crushed the landscape into those endless steam-rolled fields. It was such an unexpected confrontation that we stopped the car and leapt out, wild things across the empty road and swore right up at it. We were brave and we were nothing. (And still we are both of these things.) A little after we tell the sky to fuck off, we wind home slowly through the tiny villages. We see no other cars, few people. Sparse settlements are made up of sad-looking bungalows, as if even they've been built to bow down to the weight above. I hate the flatness for its mundanity, but the presence of the skies above it is disarming. It's just as the Polish novelist Olga Tokarczuk writes, 'That's what our houses are for – to protect us from the sky, otherwise it would pervade the very inside of our bodies . . .'.[1] Some measly protection. An old man salutes us silently and with the formality of an admiral from his front garden. The postbox outside the church, also a bungalow, is for prayers only.

These deities of ours, they came borne on the weather. The God of the Old Testament, without doubt a god of the most tempestuous meteorology (nor a god of much forgiveness, either), stands together with Zeus, Thor and Taranis. All three wielded power over the storms, had lightning bolts to their advantage and weren't afraid to use them. Oya, the West-African Yoruba spirit, has a name that translates into English as 'she tore'. And this she lives up to: sending fire, tempest and tornado to rack the lands below her in a devastating and eternal rage. Bunzi has power over the rain in Woyo mythology, as does the Vedic god Indra and the Georgian Tamar.[2]

Borne on the weather, it's true, but they swiftly outgrew it (they do grow up fast, these gods of ours). They hold it now in cupped hands. Temper and hurl it. In the days before satellites our weather systems were often unpredictable, and storms could sweep in with no forewarning to speak of. And so it's no wonder we attached the weather to higher powers like this; feeling the need to provide a reason for such destruction. We no longer blame the gods, for the most part, but what we have retained from our ancestors is the naming of our storms. This has more than just a practical use, it is more than a means of communication between governmental bodies and the general public, and I believe that it's more than a way to sell newspapers, at that. Naming something can diminish its power. Remember Storm Clara from 2011? Re-christened Hurricane Bawbag by Scottish Twitter, the name took off with such force that it was even referred to as this on the local news. And naming a storm can also turn it into something more recognisable than arbitrary destruction; something you can convince to turn the other way, something you can tame.

Regardless of who sent it, the weather can be huge and terrifying, with lightning that forks and splays across the horizon right there in front of you (all the hills turning black and so briefly illuminated). High up in the Dolomite mountains, just over the Austrian border, I once watched it flood-light a tiny smattering of houses in the squeeze of a remote valley far below me. All around a skyline of broken teeth gaped in ragged silhouette. And me, close enough to the lightning to smell it. That was power. A little while before this, my older sister and I had leapt into a glacial lake, a mirror of a thing, and our yells and yelps had bounced all the way back up the path we'd just made our way down. Another evening, and the weather in a different dress – the dusk had arrived just as we were standing on the cusp of a hill. Over the opposite peak (at a gliding creep, at a rolling tumble), was the mist. Waiting. Huge and inevitable. And then across it came; made its muscular crawl along the valley floor, thickset and broad-shouldered as any rugby player. Across it came. To us. To us. It was the closest I'd ever been to the sky, up there. Closest it had ever come to me, too.

However deep-rooted it may be in our psyches, our attempts at domestication link us back to an age in which we had a true fear of monsters, of conscious forces far greater and more powerful than ourselves (an age in which we lived in a world less explained). Though folklore and mythology is no longer in the common consciousness, our version of the world is still somewhat fantastical (the god Pan still dancing wildly across the hills of our minds). We are biologically inclined to see faces in everyday objects; our brains hardwired to recognise beings similar to ourselves in trees, clouds and rocks – predisposing us to imagine gods and spirits in the natural world.[3] Believing in monsters has never been our fault, just another quirk in our neurological design. And so just as we always have done, by naming our storms today we are continuing in this trope of creating our own meteorological monsters. In some small way, we are slotting ourselves back into the global family tree.

The fact is, this is something inevitable. Whether we are feeling it or not, we are the people of *now*. But like rivers or mycelium pathways or the roots of a tree that has remained standing for centuries and will remain for centuries more, there is an interconnectedness between us and our ancestors that jars with the singularity and hierarchical nature of contemporary life. And in exploring how better to experience the now, I've come to realise that there's something in opening it up to include the people who have been living in it, in all of the times before me. Our family here is endless and don't you forget it; stretches back across a timespan you on your own are far too small to comprehend. They didn't take much with them though, when they left, which is for the best. Because it means we get to meet them daily through all our ancient objects, through landscapes once occupied and long-since abandoned (where past and present sit tight as geological strata). And they exist through the absorption of art, too. Much the same as looking out across an emptied valley, or any space once occupied by busy human presence, art, as we've already discussed, contains all of it. So much time passed in that one unmoving image. And that family of ours, it'll stretch forwards too. Here's hoping.

And all under the same skies, at that.

And so one evening, with another blazing sunset just past, and only a few miles outside of Cambridge, this is just where I find myself. I sit down on a boardwalk that's been constructed over the boggy fens, zigzagging its way ahead of me across the wide expanse of marshland. To my left, the narrow waterway is lined with feathery reeds, the peaty water in a rich mahogany. I am wearing a dress and midges fly up from the marsh underneath the boards and bite me on the backs of my thighs. Much later I read that in the eighteenth century, malaria-infected midge bites were thought to cure melancholy. Lacklustre patients would be sent to East Anglia to contract the disease.[4] Malaria or no malaria, a midge bite certainly gives you something else to focus on.

Just as dusk begins to really descend, there is a moment of absolutely nothing. When the sky sheds all of its inhabitants and the world is cloaked in a vast and daunting emptiness. When even the tyre screech of the midges seems to dim. In this moment the clouds are bluer than the sky and the sky white. And in this moment too, under this great and all-encompassing void,

I wonder, briefly, what I am doing here, alone again and in the still and nebulous half-light. Because so often to be a woman is to balance uncomfortably between desiring solitude and fearing it. And so often to be a woman is to not understand where the fear comes from, until you do.

Stillness, though, out here and under the skies, does not last long. All around is crawling, skittering, squirming. The earth spins and wobbles on its axis. Life at nightfall continues at its usual hectic pace, even for those whose existence spans mere millimetres. Seated as I am on the boardwalk, and in this position no taller than the fenland grasses that surround me, I find myself right in among it – all this life on such minute scale. We know that social media displaces the self, which can exacerbate a sense of dissociation. But what about when we are *distracted* away from the self instead? What then? My research into the self has led me to believe that reality sits someplace distant, a place where *nosce te ipsum* is all just irrelevance; not a finding more of myself, but instead a turning away from it. And I wonder again, do you not really begin to be alive until you have lost yourself completely? It's here I find the answer. It is all somewhat of a distraction from the bigger picture of what I have come here to do (looking to the skies, surely that's the biggest thing of all?). But this is a distraction that feels far different to anything short-term and online, any of the distractions I put to paper in Chapter II. Distracted away from the internal, I find myself instead slipping into reality. In just the same way as happens when in the flow state, I find that by focusing my attention elsewhere, the world around me draws itself close. I am here, distracted into the present, immersed in the most minuscule of moments. It is an active rather than a passive distraction; a *noticing*, more than anything else.

There are innumerable things to pay attention to, we all know this. But just as much of an issue is when we stop paying attention at all. This is known as habituation: the neural process that stops us responding to anything that we have become used to. The process of habituation helps the brain to conserve energy by curbing focus on the things we know to be safe or familiar, and staying hypervigilant only for the possible threats. But it does come with a downside. We can habituate to *anything* familiar to us: from the furniture and artwork in our homes, the dishes that we loved when we first cooked them, to the outfits we once obsessed over and saved up for. All now normal. All now boring. But what about if we somehow *unaccustomed* ourselves? Could we, just in the noticing, turn our worlds into something constantly intriguing and new?[5]

I doubt the seventeenth-century French philosopher Blaise Pascal was thinking about New Year's Eve when he wrote about the contradiction between anticipation and arrival, but it works just as well. Often, when the present moment finally gets here, it doesn't quite live up to our expectations, and so we reject it. The present speeds past us and we turn our gaze instead to the future. This isn't only the case if the present moment disappoints us, but also if it bores or (as we've already discussed) stresses us out. We can't stop time, Pascal tells us, but we can control the way we move through it.[6] *Perhaps, then*, I wonder, *I don't need to rely on the moments in which I'm thrown headfirst into the present, I just need to anchor myself in. Focus.* And so this is exactly what I do.

As dusk folds itself deeper into the sky, the tonality of my surroundings (my own clothes and skin) deepens too. There is the breeze through the grasses and the clear cut of water, borne from the body of a leaping fish. I lie down right where I am on the slatted path. The wood is soft and warm against my skin and above me is a sky written in a language I have never learnt. The stars.

The stars. I am far from the first to search for meaning in the night sky. Humans have been interpreting the stars for millennia; and for millennia have worshipped celestial beings, have found omens, fates and fortunes through a process no more difficult than the upward tilt of a head. And since prehistory we've all of us been mapping stars onto the walls of caves and painting the heavens in exquisite astrological detail inside the domed roofs of Renaissance palaces. Even today, an enormous constellation on a peacock-green background graces the ceiling of New York's Grand Central Station. See, for the past 20,000 years, not only have we been using the stars to orientate ourselves on earth, but also to find our place within the universe – using the language of the heavens as a reassurance of how and where we fit.

The Lascaux cave complex in the Dordogne is filled with an extraordinary stampede of prehistoric creatures: three hundred and sixty-four horses, ninety stags, numerous cattle and bison, big cats, one rhino, a bear. Here you see a pair of bison. They stand one behind the other so that their legs are crossing over each other; a composition that displays a 20,000-year-old ability in the use of perspective.[7] It is a breathtaking display of palaeolithic artistry. The parade stretches right to the upper reaches of the rooms – creatures no longer terrestrial, but sprung from the earth and floating.[8] Hooves hang in empty space. If this cave is anything to go by, it appears that there have been strange beasts in the sky ever since our ancestors first lifted their heads and noticed it.

And the stars, they're here too. Six circular dots above the left shoulder of a muscular aurochs, the wild ancestor of our modern domestic cattle. These are the Pleiades, the star grouping that today marks out one corner of our own bull constellation, known to us as Taurus. But *this* beast, set amidst its skybound menagerie, is his predecessor. Here, the exact same stars make up the same creature, many thousands of years before the Ancient Greeks bestowed him their new and modern name. They have kept pace with our own evolution, the occupants of this celestial zoo, creeping into our mythologies and shape-shifting accordingly. Myth turns into myth turns into myth. They're closer to home now though, our myths. We have social media to mythologise the self, and Instagram filters that mythologise the body. News outlets, political spin, hate speech – these are all forms of myth, too. Fiction today lies far closer than the heavens.

I haven't been interested in star signs since I was about fourteen. Recently, however, through a heady mix of procrastination and clickbait, I seem to be unable to spend a day in front of my computer without checking my horoscope (myriad interruptions cascade onto my desk). My new boyfriend is a Libra, like me, and though I pretend to myself I am doing it ironically, I look up our compatibility ratings. Which, on every website I check on, turn out to be 'OK'. My reaction to this is unironic. Especially as we apparently hold the shared trait of falling in love easily. We have done, and I am unable to shake off the feeling that being in a Libra/Libra relationship is little more than settling for what you got.

People turn to astrology for all kinds of reasons, but most interestingly for us here is its use as a coping mechanism. See, evidence suggests that more people become interested in their horoscopes during tumultuous historical periods; astrological readings bringing a sense of reassurance and certainty during uncertain times. An influx of articles, for example, were published in the US about astrology during the Great Depression of the

1930s, and in Germany between the two World Wars.[9] And a resurgence in interest has certainly come synonymous with the stress and anxiety of recent years; I know I'm not the only one (and by one, please read 'millennial') with this new-found fascination in looking to the stars. According to Google Trends, searches for both 'birth chart' and 'astrology' hit five-year peaks in 2020, and have remained high (as I'm sure you can imagine) ever since.[10] In the words of religious anthropologist Dr Susannah Crockford of Ghent University, astrology appeals to so many of us because the general population are 'anxiously spending too much time online, alone, thinking about themselves and what is going on in the world . . .'.[11] Well that sounds about right.

In the fractured chaos of our world today, I find there is something strangely reassuring in visualising deep space; in imagining those slow cycles grinding on, accurate and unfailing, in all that vast darkness. Astrology is a knowledge gleaned far from the news; a knowledge that feels far bigger and somehow more trustworthy than anything we have here on earth at the moment. But it isn't the only age-old system we use to unravel the nature of our own existence.

In New York I get my tarot read in a purple one-room establishment called Psychic and Crystal. Inside is a purple-and-gold-patterned carpet and purple-and-gold Rococo-style furniture and huge lumps of purple crystal on the table, split down the middle and glowing. I sit on a dirty white chair outside the front of the shop while the psychic finishes up a palm reading. The day never really got going and so dusk has fallen easy; the heavy white sky giving over to blue-grey and headlights. The shop fronts across the road from me glow an inviting yellow. Snow has been falling intermittently since I left the hotel that morning, and it's only gotten colder since; ice on the wind. Blowing on my hands, I glance inside. The psychic is not looking at her client's palm, instead she is playing with a pair of headphones, winding them mindlessly in and out of her fingers. Fluorescent light glares down on the scene.

The psychic is young and called Diamond. She is wearing her pyjamas.

Cleave me apart like one of those glinting crystals and now I know that you would find me composed of the following: of lucky numbers one and three, and lucky days Tuesday and Thursday. You'd find the future inside me as well, all tangled up together with my attributes and failings (which repel each other like the same pole on a pair of magnets and give me stomachache). Scraps of hard-gleaned history, too; no such thing as water under the bridge in this establishment. I am destined, to my not entirely joyful surprise, to have three babies, but will fall pregnant only twice. A house move is on the horizon and although my current partner has soulmate potential he finds it difficult to vocalise his feelings for me (an easy-win being that that's the majority of all men). I have been hurt by a narcissist and suffered trauma between the ages of nine and eleven. I need to meditate but struggle to stay focused. My mother and I are not spiritually connected due to an event that happened while I was in the womb. A powerful woman will give me bad career advice and I am advised not to listen to her. I have a spiritual void (noticed once again – I wonder if it has grown?). Some of this is true.

The psychic spills her information quickly and so quietly it is both hard to hear her and to keep up with anything that I do. No room is left for questions. I look at her slippers while she offers to cure me for an extra two hundred dollars. Declining, I leave the shop, my spiritual void bared to the freezing street like a fresh bruise.

The truth I gleaned from my reading, if I'm being a sceptic, is down to something known as the Barnum Effect: this tendency of ours to think totally generalised statements, when told to us directly, are about us, squeezing them into our personal narratives in any way we can. Still, there's a reassurance that comes with the feeling of being seen like this, however farcical it may turn out to be (and easier for us all if it is, as I doubt I will either have the money, time or inclination to have three children at any point in the near future, at least).

It's contradictory, because it's probably bullshit, but there is something that feels more authentic about all of this. And whether or not it's true doesn't really matter anyhow, because it is so easy to believe in without *really* believing in. Unlike religion, these methods demand absolutely nothing of us; they allow us to be (and even better, to make excuses for being) generally a bit of a fuck up. It's all in the translation. Both tarot and astrology allow us to tap into ourselves with an introspection rarely found elsewhere in day-to-day life. And this is an introspection we don't have to pay for or suddenly find out we need some extra equipment to take part in (like getting halfway through an online yoga class and being told to pick up your block). Of course we do pay for it though, because this is 2023. But there's a simplicity here. With tarot, all we need to do is choose a few cards. Astrology goes one step further: instead of cards, it hands us a set of characteristics, particular to us and anyone born within our celestial remit. And knowing that we are set in this way means that we can pretty much excuse ourselves for any of our chosen behaviours. There's that narrative of the self again. Whether it's astrology or anything else, we all need something to tie ourselves together, to tie ourselves down.

You see it really does keep us grounded, the sky. Right where I am lying, far into the fens, I know that a hundred miles south-west, the Uffington White Horse is looking up at the same stars. She is a cuttle-boned creature, draped over the brow of an Oxfordshire hill as if dropped there in a frozen gallop. There are siblings, too: all of them younger and who've never strayed far from their big sister; scraped hills dotted all over the British Isles reveal the shining white bones of gigantic creatures, cut from the earth some 3,000 years ago. This is a family of far inappropriate proportions for human comprehension. Makes you wonder who they were made for.

Less obscure an audience can be found in Jan van Eyck's *Virgin Annunciate* panel on the exterior of the Ghent altarpiece. Here we find her kneeling, said Virgin, thick robes gathered around a body far too big for any interior (and in so many soft folds). The Holy Ghost as dove has rested lightly on her head, though the Virgin's expression gives nothing away of having noticed. 'AVE GRATIA,' the angel Gabriel says on the panel opposite. His greeting comes in neat golden script. Kneeling too, he holds lilies – the flowers of the Annunciation. But the Virgin knows the message has not come from this flaxen-haired being, and when she speaks, her custard face tilted upwards, she directs her own words to the sky. 'ECCE ANCILLA D(OMI)NI.' 'Behold, the handmaiden of the Lord.' The words have been inscribed upside down: the message relayed neither to Gabriel, nor to us as the painting's audience, but directly to the heavens. Bit smoggy for that today, though.

An association between the heavens and, well, Heaven, really began in ancient Greek and Roman mythology; you don't have to look far to find individuals unlucky in life being immortalised as constellations. And as a concept it's hardly been lost to the mists of time, it's even in *The Lion King*. This pagan relationship between spirit and stars branched over the years into a multi-faith understanding that searching the skies could bring one closer to god (however one chooses to translate the word). And when the Romanian religious historian Mircea Eliade made his world-encompassing survey in the first half of the twentieth century, he found that religious experiences were consistently driven by the sky. (Incidentally, as I am writing these words I have just heard a whole crowd outside my bedroom window shout 'Hallelujah!' I'm not sure how exactly to interpret this.) And on the secular side of things, astronauts returning from space often describe something known as the 'Overview Effect' – a term that describes a shift in perspective on seeing our small home planet from such a distance. Astronauts talk about how it was all there and right below them: all human and animal life, shooting stars and the aurora borealis, and everything down there in the deepness of the oceans. All there, and so fragile, too.

What Eliade discovered in his megalith of research, however, was that it wasn't just the stars instigating religious experience, it was light as well. The eighteenth-century Jesuit priest Jean Pierre de Caussade called it the sacrament of the present moment.[12] And it *is* true that light offers an immediacy to any scene, an inclusivity too. Light brings it all together and into the same instant. (Light like painting then; the capture of that one single moment – the tying together of all those fragmented narratives).

In Siracusa, on the island of Sicily, there is a Brutalist cathedral called Il Santuario della Madonna delle Lacrime (The Sanctuary of our Lady of Tears). The building is shaped according to its name – an enormous teardrop depicted at the exact moment it has collided with the ground (imagine it, just a nanosecond later, shattering – water particles ricocheting around and drenching the thirsty scrub it stands in). But it is the interior of the building that holds particular interest for us here. Once inside, turn your gaze upwards and your eyes will be flooded by the rectangular shafts of light pouring down from glass slats in the pointed ceiling. The structure of the roof curls upwards to a central peak, and though you may feel at first as if you have inadvertently walked into somebody else's shell, this light falling down on you acts as a homing tool. It is warm and welcoming; an abstract but catch-all interpretation of the spiritual. And one that feels far more significant in today's world than any of the complex and long-dead iconographies inside so many of our other sacred spaces.

An ability to translate the stars isn't (I don't *think*) a necessity in my intention to live with a deeper reality. No great tragedy there then. I want to clarify to you here that I'm bypassing what of course I know are the many other great tragedies that come from not being able to see the stars (today, as light pollution fast envelops our planet, most people in Europe and the States are unable to even see our own home galaxy, the Milky Way).[13] But for the very particular subject of reality, the thing that *is* the tragedy here is the loss of perspective that this obstruction has brought about.

Anyhow, smog or no smog, today we don't even have to look at the sky in order to orientate ourselves on the ground. Nearly 6,000 satellites circle our planet, replacing the stars in our eyeline and beaming GPS information straight down into our cars and phones. Without even having to look out of a window, we know exactly where we are. This disparity between location and an empirical sense of place has doubtless had an effect on our grounding in the three-dimensional world. The use of GPS has allowed our physical location – the very epitome of something that should be three-dimensional (that literally is three-dimensional) – to slink over into the 2D. Far more disconcertingly, many studies have shown that when using GPS to locate ourselves in this way, the areas of the brain normally involved in navigation don't just disengage, they actually shrink.[14] And if we can't orientate ourselves in the physical world, how will we ever orientate ourselves in reality? Thick fog is one thing, but without a footing in our own solar system, what chance do we have of knowing where we really stand? We have taken a step outside of the universe to better perceive it, and now we are lost.

See, it just so happens that right now we are a little out of sync. And as an increasing amount of scientific research tells us, this is not a good thing. We share – well, we *should* share – an internal clock with our fellow inhabitants, with birds and insects and plants, right the way down to microbes (it's one of the many things that connects us with everything and everyone else). This internal clock is dependent on the natural cycles of light and temperature;[15] using them regulates all sorts of vital biological activities, from our sleeping patterns to our fertility and reproduction.[16] It is only when we work against this that existence falls slightly out of kilter. We ignore our body clocks, get depressed or physically unwell. We invent our own version of timekeeping that plays in favour of capitalism and we override the scheduling of the seasons. Our clocks and watches have nothing in common with any original method of timekeeping – sundials or any other observational devices depending solely on natural phenomena. One is human-controlled, the other looks only to the skies;[17] one changes shape with the seasons, the other ignores them. Getting up five days a week in the dark makes us feel displaced from our bodies until we spend almost a fiver on a flat white and feel sick instead. We don't slow down because where's the progress in that? And we perhaps stop feeling quite as connected to it all as we could have done in the past, feeling quite as real. Something of the rhythm is off.

We don't listen to our bodies when they tell us they're tired. And when we do listen, we make them watch five episodes of an unremarkable TV show instead of putting them right to bed. Which is terrible timekeeping, in the scheme of things.

But under these skies, this human timekeeping of ours falls into insignificance. Seeing it all awash like that, laid out there in the fens; seeing it all awash like that, past and present all above me as one; and seeing skies so huge like that and weather so dramatic – well, it does work to make me feel a little insignificant. Would do the same to you, too. And there's something comforting to that: being so tiny you could be nothing. So tiny you *are* nothing. A speck, less than, under the great mystery of these great skies.

It's true that we live in an age of knowing, but lying here makes me think there's also something in the not. Something in the belief of being looked down on by more than the vast and cold emptiness of space. 'Repopulate the cosmos!' I want to shout into the faces of everyone I see. Redefine the stars as Plato did – those divine and eternal animals.[18] Believe, like Kandinsky, in an animate universe. 'Not only the stars, moon, woods and flowers of which poets sing,' the artist once said, 'but even a cigar butt lying in the ashtray, a patient white trouser-button looking up at you from a puddle on the street, a submissive piece of bark carried through the long grass in the ant's strong jaws.'[19]

And believe, above all, that we don't just live under it, we *are* it.

Driving home from the fens later that night I get a call from the police. My car has been reported for being parked up on the side of the verge by someone in one of the scattering of houses that lines the reserve. Fear again, perhaps. Miles away an electrical storm plays out in miniature. The horizon lights up intermittently; no thunder or really any sound at all, save the insects and the distant hum of evening traffic.

❧

Sometimes the sky displays itself with more clarity than you know what to do with. Pre-storm skies in chiaroscuro and everything all a mix. As if it's saying to you, 'You don't have to choose; here it all is. Right now and all at once. Take it, it'll be gone in an instant. Take it before the rain starts.'

You only need to open a door to get to it, or a window even. Do it. Look up and the stars are out. Final drops of rain but just the sound of it, slight and only if you listen hard. All outside sharply aware compared to the cotton-wool warmth of your kitchen. Later the stars appear and you can feel there's something about the place calling in the frost. The kind of cold that feels geometric. The kind of cold that sharpens your edges and tells you that you are here. And more importantly, that you are.

It does get you, the weather. Sometimes it taps at your window when you're not expecting a visitor at all. The wind can make you reckless, golden light on the grass and the trees so loud-spoken with their non-stop rustling. Everything and everyone alive and flurious. Impossible to even have a conversation in all the cacophony. And the waving grasses (fluff and pale greenness) catch people's shadows and play with them, distorting images and passing them along and along. The ripples on the river fast-moving, the clouds in buffeted scuds. Clouds that make you wonder why you ever go back inside your head. There's this strand of early Christianity that imagines the mind of Adam to have been fashioned from clouds – an unstable, undelineated material (which explains a lot, if the same goes for ours).[20] And when, in Norse mythology, the giant Ymir (whose name translates from Old Norse as 'screamer') is murdered, his brains are flung into the air where strands of it hang as them.[21] A perfect example of closed-circuit recycling.

There are all sorts of clouds that feel more substantial than you do, sometimes. These are the sorts of clouds that Constable painted. Looking straight up and capturing an impression more than anything, and more than that capturing a sense of him right out there in the fields with his paints. I was once given a hundred hand-printed postcards of one of his cloud studies. The painting's been printed the wrong way up on all of them and whenever I write on their backs I imagine Constable lying there looking upside down at the scene, cropped wheat rough-pressed into his spine.

There he is. At home and under it.

I want reality to howl through me like the wind

VIII

Homesick

HARD TO FEEL LONELY, what with the company of all those stars. And the darkness in-between wrapping me all up in it – wrapping all of us up together (me and you – it's not that we even know each other). Here we are warm and endless in reams of thick deep velvet. It's surely true the night sky makes us all feel at home, wherever we happen to be.

I first began to interrogate the meaning of home when I spent a month with a friend cycling across the States. Long alien days spent in a trilogy of geometry and colour – blue sky, ochre desert, the vertical cut of a straight grey road; the landscape three-point perspective at its most simple. We were, for that time, without home; moving slow across the country motel to motel, each room ours for eight hours at best. And for that whole month we existed among strangers: holidaymakers, business people, crumpled families with their entire life loaded up in the back of a truck. It was Christian, the desert. Huge signs that praised God all along the miles of empty roadside, eternal salvation promised to the sand (the arms of the cacti ever raised in adulation).

Temptation knocking? Let Jesus get the door!
If life makes it hard to stand, kneel
What is missing in ch ch? UR!

That whole journey, we spent a lot of time in Starbucks; sitting on plastic chairs in plastic bungalows like growths among the craters of the strange and surrounding landscape. There were fast-food joints too: all bright fluorescent lights and synthetic cheer. None of it felt like home. I looked out of the window at the orange and blue nothing and never felt so lost.

Nostalgia is a Greek word, translating, quite literally, as the suffering evoked by a desire to return to one's place of origin; the pain of wanting to go home. Originally diagnosed as a sickness, the term was coined in 1668 by Swiss physician Johannes Hofer. He used it to describe the acute physical pain expressed by Swiss mercenaries stationed in the lowlands of Italy and longing for home. It's a romantic notion, to want something so hard it makes you sick, and one taken so seriously back then that playing a particular Swiss milking song was punishable by death, for fear it would rile up the soldiers.

This original translation meant that, all the way through the seventeenth and eighteenth centuries, nostalgia was thought to only affect the Swiss. In fact, it was only in the early nineteenth century that it began to be acknowledged as a widespread condition – a form of melancholy or depression.[1] And the alleged symptoms *are* similar to those of melancholia: fainting, high temperatures, hallucinations. Indigestion. Coined as it was in the seventeenth century, however, references to the actual *feeling* of nostalgia can be found as far back as antiquity. We're only human; always missing something or other.

If one could actually stand back and take a look at it, nostalgia would be more of an overlay to place, more a watercolour wash than anything hard or physical. It's existence in layers. With nostalgia at play, nothing can exist as it is, and place differs with every individual perception of it. It's no wonder, then, that reality is hard to come by (no wonder other people's can seem so bizarre either). We've all experienced them: those moments so sudden and imbued with longing you can barely function. And maybe you don't even know what the longing was for; it could come from a line of poetry, or the momentary shadow of a flock of birds against the side of an office block. It could come from a smell, or the texture of a certain kind of fabric. Or from a glimpse into somebody else's life (perhaps that one you feel you should be leading instead – where is yours? Who has it?). It's in these moments that the feeling tears into you and leaves just as quick. And there you are – left now with an ache, with some gaping hole evident only to you. And there you stand like a lightning-struck tree, cleaved but still upright (just). The empty space that spills right out of you.

Because we are arts graduates – and fresh ones too – nobody seems that keen to employ us. And so my friend and I have volunteered on a poorly filled charity relay stretching almost 3,000 miles across the States, from San Francisco to New York. Someone in the office back in the UK has the idea for us to buy a bike to cycle the stretches that nobody wants to run. Which turns out to be almost the entirety of the Midwest. Our modest budget allows us to buy one bike only (and hardly a bike at that – in the first shop we go to with our paltry sum the manager tells us to try Toys 'R' Us instead). Having only one bike means that, despite being together on this vast continent, we make our shared journey entirely alone. Every day, one of us will remain in the car, watching the curve of the other's back as they pedal away towards the horizon: a figure getting smaller and smaller down an inscrutably straight road, turning into waved heat, and then nothing at all. Each day meanders around the other and we do the same, leapfrogging each other slowly via our two means of transportation. We live off coffee and high-sugar peanut butter and avocado sandwiches, and fortune cookies that we snap open in our many times of crisis. The wind is always against us, making even the steep downhills an effort. My friend consistently gets chased by stray dogs and we fall out because I convince him to cycle on the freeway and he almost gets hit by a truck.

Most places we go, we get asked why we are there. By and large, this is always done in a friendly capacity. But it's a difficult question even so, and we never know quite how to reply as we are increasingly unsure of the answer ourselves. One afternoon we go to a tiny cafe in some straight line town in the middle of the desert. The proprietor – on hearing our accents, and so quickly that I almost miss it – hisses to her colleague right out of one side of her mouth: 'Get the cards.' Her face remains almost completely unchanged as she does this, filled with the same beaming hospitality she greeted us with as soon as we came through the door. I've never seen a person split themselves so successfully and immediately in this way, neither before nor since. And when we go to leave, there is a rack of postcards, curling with age, displayed right beside the entrance.

I'd been dreaming of home. And always in a similar setting. Always the ocean close by. And always I would wake up homesick for a place I had never once visited, and, worse, was unsure even existed. If dreams are the subconscious communicating with the conscious mind,[2] as we're told they are, then my own seemed to be making things pretty clear. It's just that it kept forgetting to leave the address. I would wake up from these dreams with the feeling I'd been thrown out of my home as ignominiously as Adam and Eve from the Garden of Eden. Draught from the door slammed behind me giving me the chills.

You'd find the two of them – Adam and Eve, that is – best depicted marching out from a corner at the very top of Masaccio's Brancacci Chapel in Florence. This is their punishment, really. It's not that they had to leave, though that was bad enough – it's that they are eternally in the shameful process of it. (I'd be more interested in seeing what happened next. I'd like to see them opening a shared bank account, adopting a kitten, lugging an abandoned piece of furniture up many flights of stairs to a dimly lit flat with a mould problem.) Eve's eyes, mouth, have been painted as nothing more than (or nothing less than, maybe) a violent rip in the pallid flat of her face. Raised up to a God who no longer wants her.

Religion never gave me much either, I'd like to tell her. I've often felt that I've been walking repeatedly into a hard surface; there for it all, but with it never quite accepting me. It did the exact opposite, actually. Something (someone?) spoke to me once. I'd been in this tiny ancient church: one of those bare, thickset buildings, stark and hugging all at the same time. There were dark marks on the walls where the damp had once come in, and I was there standing at a varnished pew, repeating words I held no belief in. And a voice: not mine nor that of anyone around me, but as loud and clear as if it had come into my ear direct from my closest neighbour. *Get out, get out, get out*, it said. And so I did. I stood under the yew among the graves outside and waited for the service to end – the tree old as the church, darker, more imposing. *Get out, get out, get out.* Not for me, none of it.

The landscape dries up as my friend and I make our slow way across the country, creeping so high that our water bottles twist with the change in air pressure and we are left light-headed and breathless. Everywhere we look we see unfriendly cacti and scrubby trees that scream up out of the dirty-orange craters. There are flat-topped rock formations and green-blue shrubs and the sky and the burning heat. After that, nothing but space; so vast it's almost impossible to comprehend. And out there on a bike you could be the only person alive (certainly you will be the only one on a bike). And, most days, because the clouds are so low and the horizon so far distant – the road so undeniably and unendingly straight – it makes me feel as if I exist in a long and narrow box. Cushioned in my solitude and unable to escape. There's tumbleweed too, though even now I still can't quite believe in it. And eagles that swoop low in the road in front of us; bright sun shining through the tips of their wings.

I spent much of my early twenties attempting to be spiritual in one way or another. And if we go by the scientific and psychological research alone, these attempts came for good reason. To name just a few of its positive physical effects, religion has been linked to lower rates of cancer, heart disease and blood pressure, which means fewer strokes too. And when religious people *do* get ill, better immune functioning means improved outcomes for infections like HIV and meningitis, as well as faster recovery from other illnesses and both minor and major surgeries. Religious people tend to age better too, making them at lower risk of age-related cognitive decline and physical impairment.

There are less miraculous reasons for the above. In a physical capacity, religious people tend to lead healthier lifestyles all round. As a generalisation, they smoke and drink less, if at all. This tends to be coupled with less promiscuity and unprotected sex, and attending religious services leads people away from loneliness (with its psychological and physical ill effects) and to stronger and more regular social bonding. And with more people around to spot it, in these regular social scenarios, ill health tends to get caught earlier and dealt with more successfully. Religious people tend to have lower stress levels too – which may also answer the lessened cancer risk and higher immune responses (both intrinsically linked to stress). And what about this advanced rate of healing? That's evidence of the placebo effect. In other words, believing you will be cured may well actually work to cure you.[3]

Despite not knowing this until now, I have sat in halls all over the world attempting to feel things, suspicious that all the emotions I could not source had already been soaked up by the people around me. I have introduced myself as many different colours, and slightly fewer times as types of weather. I am blue-grey and cloudy. I am terracotta. I am moss-green like a forest floor. I am the eye of a storm. I am humid. I am the selfish rain that comes horizontal and only in Glasgow. (I am never purple.) I have whispered my deepest secret into the ears of a stranger and my even deeper one into the wall beside them. I have listened to a secret that I blurted out to my housemates as soon as I got back to our flat, and have never really stopped feeling guilty about since. I have silently apologised to my child self and to both my sisters and to my mother. I have drunk a lot of herbal tea.

And though I was told off so aggressively that time in the church by I don't know what, I do keep feeling I am missing out on something. When I look back at my chapter themes it hits me that so much of what brings me into the real can also be found within an ecclesiastical or spiritual context. Landscape, sky, touch, water, painting – all of these sensory experiences that turn us towards the divine, I've found to also work in turning me back to myself.

It was since the Enlightenment, really, that religion moved to the backseat. There it sauntered in, the Enlightenment, eloquent and measured and with a focus only on the rational, laying down a rule-based and causal interpretation of the world and universe.[4] And as religion stepped out of the limelight, so too did the moral code that faith gives us to live by, and the firm standing that comes with it inside our known universe. But we're still looking for ways out of it, the universe. The metaverse, for those who care, appears to neatly slot into the gap left by religion. Unsatisfied with this life, we are waiting in hope for the next – we've heard that one before. The metaverse is immersive but not yet completely so, and inside your headset you might hear unwanted noise from other people's domesticities seeping in as you chat to them in the ether; both of you trying to ignore the other's whining children, noisy pet, or distant traffic.

It's not that we want rules exactly, but a lack of guidance does seem to have left us wandering. It's no wonder that so many of us are on the search once again for alternative belief systems.[5] And so it's at this juncture that I have to ask myself whether religion *is* actually the answer; whether all this soul-searching has been, well, literally just that. We can't exist only by the cold and hard and rational. In a world led by science, we're looking for something more, we're looking for *meaning*.

The Texas Panhandle brings forth bursts of colour – all kinds of different grasses and wildflowers to either side of us, whole fields of them in constant motion with the winds; more like the movement of water than anything else. Small birds fly up out of the fields every so often and one I follow for half a mile or so. It flies parallel to me and just in front, stopping every so often on the fence posts for me to catch up. Far beyond the both of us, the landscape has darkened right down into tones of blue (a visual phenomenon that Leonardo had recognised almost five hundred years previous, looking out across the hills of Tuscany). Later, my friend's turn on the bike and mine in the car, I drive past a cowboy washing his horse by hose. There are tortoises all over the road and because nearly every other animal we've seen has been dead (all crushed roadkill with their eyes popping out of their skulls like in a cartoon), I stop for them repeatedly and carry them across.

Vultures circling above. Miles further on, seeds from the cottonwoods have drifted into soft masses all over the road. Everything gauzelike.

In Cincinnati we meet a triathlete granny and her eight-year-old daughter, also a triathlete. In the park they are running through, I hear but cannot see the reason for a small boy shouting 'Dad, Dad! Come and look at me punching this deer in the face!'

At time of writing, earth is on the verge of another mass extinction; the sixth, but the first and only that will have been caused by one of the world's native species – that's us. I don't think any of us are able to deny that we are scared. And even if this is a fear deep-hidden in the subconscious (like so much else), we all know to varying extents what is happening to our planet. And even if this is a fear that manifests itself as something totally other – an unfounded anxiety that interrupts our sleep as rudely awakening as an alarm; or an intrusive thought that wedges itself, like a land-slidden rock, against a musing on a totally different subject – it is fear nonetheless. This fear, it's huge and abstract and we do not want to face it. How could we be so arrogant as to believe we had mastery over all of this? I think of my dreams of home and how it is that they are always dreams of nature. And as I write this I hold in my mind the images I woke up with behind my eyes this morning: a bright beach, winter sun on the water and I think what must have been the New York skyline in the near distance; and, all the way along it, orcas had washed to shore, their white throats slit and the flesh inside deep tuna-red. Blood all mixed up with the sand. There were crows too (or rooks or ravens, I'm always unsure), hundreds of them flying overhead. I opened my eyes with a missing, a breaking, a feeling I'd arrived too late. There was a telling (something, certainly, was said).

Nostalgia, as those poor Swiss soldiers knew, was something that came synonymous with longing, with that tough realisation of a life divided – the now set apart from the then. The future, increasingly terrifying, acquiesces to the past (whose horrors we didn't know personally, and so find far easier to ignore). But if we spend so much of our time there, in a past that was possibly never even ours in the first place, surely as much as we are reminiscing, we are dismissing the present too?

We've already spoken about fear. About how it can be one of the many natural reasons we dissociate. And I wonder if, in terms of the planet, this fear has created some kind of vicious cycle: that we have dissociated because we are scared, and that because we are scared we have dissociated. But here's the thing, how about if this feeling was actually just as easily simplified? We can't deny modern science. It's correct; we are tiny, we may be temporary, and the planet does not need us. Not as we are right now, in any case. But this mess of misunderstanding and misattributed emotion is really only asking us one thing – to reconnect. Twentieth-century science has told us that we have nothing in common with our planet, but perhaps our century, the twenty-first, is going to lead us en masse to believe the reverse. By living in a society that disallows a connection to the earth and universe to be a crucial part of our existence, we'd be hard-pressed not to find ourselves sometimes removed and lonely. See, we have been led to believe that to be a human being is to profit and to own. And because we live in a world in which it is increasingly difficult to do either, we have been led to believe that we have failed instead. But if it is true that we are a population disconnected from the earth, then surely all we need to do to break this cycle is to learn to dig into it (because it can only be fact that there is nothing richer than soil after the rain). 'You can't be present all the time,' the poet Kae Tempest tells us, 'but the closer we focus on our experience, the greater the awareness of the experience will be, the greater the immersion, the greater the possibility for connection.'[6]

That's not to say this reconnection doesn't come with difficulty. For many of us, this relationship, this connection with the planet, we never even had the chance to have it in the first place. This ugly issue is one of privilege. We've already touched on the many issues surrounding access to our water systems, and the same goes for land. With half of England still owned by one percent of the population, we live in a gated-off landscape; penned in, as the activist and writer Nick Hayes tells us, to 'the illusion that the value of the land is unconnected to the community around it'.[7] It's not ours, we're told, and never was. Landscape, and the reality that comes with it, has become a privilege, not a right. The screen spreads, slowly. But it's not all gloomy. It feels crucial here to mention the huge number of community groups, activists and radical individuals who are and have been working tirelessly in attempting to highlight and combat many of the issues I have put down on paper in the process of writing this book. You are the people holding the gaps of the spreading screen before they close completely, shutting off the entrance between us and true reality. You are the people holding open the space for us to climb through. Your arms must be tired with all the strain, and so I thank all of you who are doing this, in whatever way you are doing it.

Connection is *crucial* for the feeling we are after. We need to tie ourselves back in. Because though the planet may not need *us*, we need *it*. And if we reintegrate, if we re-engage, perhaps by helping it, we can help ourselves too. All we need is a retranslation of the contradiction we've all found ourselves in, just for the simple fact of existing – the earth being something we've all just somehow ended up on, but at the same time also our home. Both these statements are equally true.

And how about this contradiction we live in – how about we lean into it? Alone, we are tiny, insignificant specks – that much is true. And we are reminded of this as much in a spiritual context as we are when immersed in the outside world, or when looking at an artwork or when experiencing anything at all we find to be incomprehensible and majestic. Yes, we are minuscule, yet this enormous, undecipherable, unimaginable universe is our home. This knowledge can only be awe-inspiring.

Three weeks later we get to New York, where we stay a few nights with an old friend. When we arrive there is a small ceremony in Prospect Park and it's our job to make a triumphant sprint onto the outdoor stage, our relay baton held proud and aloft. The audience files in past us as we try to hide behind the Portaloos. Later, the friend we are staying with takes us to a beautiful soap shop on Broadway with a huge stone font right in the middle of the room. We stand on the steps and have our hands washed by the staff, which makes us laugh and then both burst unexpectedly into floods of tears.

ABOUT AWE

(a small interlude)

I AM LYING, once again, in the dark; this time stretched out on the marble floor of the chapel of San Marco in Venice. Flat on my back on this cold and uncomfortable surface, I gaze up into the black and wait for someone to turn the lights on. And when they do, they flicker first into the furthest reaches of the space, coming closer and closer and then overhead (the interior is enormous, and even the sound of the light switches are party to its excellent acoustics). If you were there next to me, you'd notice how the light displays itself slowly across the space, and with an effect that would make you turn to me and agree that, yes, you could almost call it layered. And halfway through this ecclesiastical light show you might, as I do, imagine that you are lying in space completely candlelit. This effect doesn't last, though, and before long there it all is: the entire space illuminated, the mosaics of the domed gold ceiling and every surface of every wall below it, right there in your eyes and not about to go anywhere either. The whole place feels like an intake of breath. It's as if the chapel has stored them up, somehow – the obligatory gasp of each person who's walked in (the sound lives as a feeling and hasn't yet stopped growing). It *is* brilliant, in every definition of the word: a blaze of light and saints and angels; piety mocked and set in twenty-four-carat gold. Jesus is wearing blue and an uncomfortable-looking pair of leather sandals. He stares resolutely ahead from his throne in the dome of the main apse, seemingly determined not to notice the group of quietly weeping art history students I have brought with me (making tiny and messy additions to the complex patterns of the floor below him).

I look around me, at all this brilliance, and feel absolutely nothing.

See, though awe can strike thick and fast as the weather, it can just as easily pass you by entirely. Helps to look out for it, though admittedly this can often be difficult: our phones pull our gaze downwards[1] and our society makes it hard to focus attention on anything but ourselves. This constant preoccupation with the self, this 'me, me, me' culture, cuts us off from the rest of the world and can make us isolated, anxious and absorbed. And if we're neither looking up nor out enough, we lose our greatest opportunity to experience it. As Mircea Eliade discovered through his research on religious experience, awe's most longstanding trigger is the sky, in all of its capacities. (Here's a question for you – have you ever seen fireworks in the daytime? How they are nothing but noise and thick bursts of smoke. And how the smoke just hangs there still and heavy in the air, as if by some miracle?) Stress blinkers us too: stops us noticing the things outside of our heads, and when we do all we see are hindrances blown right out of proportion. And though awe can be found in other people, sometimes this is just as easily replaced in our heads with jealousy instead.

But there *are* those moments where you cannot even begin to fathom how a feeling so vast got into that small body of yours. We've already spoken about that; that overwhelm of something more beautiful than you could ever have prepared yourself for, or far larger than your sense of self. And it's this magnificent 'oneness', this 'more than' that's thought to be at the core of religious experience[2] – which makes sense, as all built up like this we might finally be big enough to stand eye to eye with any excuse of a god. Awe is a feeling of such inexplicability that even if afterwards you find yourself a rational explanation – can pin your experience down to an unusual meteorological occurrence, an impossible natural landscape or a piece of art or architecture – the feeling of wonderment, the all-encompassing and closed-book riddling of it, remains unshakeable.

We've been feeling awestruck for thousands of years, but its effects have only really been properly researched for the last twenty of them. In an enormous study headed by Berkeley Professor of Psychology Dacher Keltner, experiencing awe has been found to provide all kinds of benefits for our physical and mental wellbeing. Keltner and his research team found that after experiencing it in any capacity, their volunteers felt happier and less stressed for weeks afterwards. Awe has been proven to break habitual or negative thought patterns and make experiencers more invested and interested in the outside world (interestingly, similar to the effects of magic mushrooms). This research has not only proven that awe activates the parasympathetic nervous system – which, as we know, calms the fight-or-flight response[3] – but that experiencing it also has a positive effect on the vagus nerve (the system that, discussed in Chapter II, is massively affected in response to stress).[4] The list goes on, but I want to find out something far more specific. I want to know why awe has the power to make me feel more real.

And to do so, we have to return, once again, to the self. See, awe and the self have a direct relationship to one another. As part of his research, Keltner asked the participants of his study group to draw themselves and sign their names, before and after experiencing awe. After an experience of awe, he found that every member of the study group both drew themselves *and* signed their names smaller, leading him to hypothesise that experiencing awe actually shrinks our sense of self.[5] This is known in psychological terms as 'self-diminishment': a quieting of the self (or whatever we deem to be the self, anyhow). And losing that sense of self, or quieting it at least (as I came to discover in my experiments with floatation) allows us to focus on an existence outside of our heads. Awe shifts us away from self-interest and our day-to-day concerns and instead, by jolting us into the sharp focus of something we are far too small to comprehend (in its totality, at least), allows us to gain some sense of perspective on the wider picture. But what is most interesting in the context of our particular topic is that Keltner's volunteers, consistently and in multiple studies, used the word 'connection' when describing the after-effects of experiencing awe. Awe, he discovered, can pull us away from our usual self-referential states and increase 'prosocial' behaviour – the kinds of behaviours that see us help other people: like being more generous, compassionate or co-operative, for example.[6] And not only this, but experiencing awe moved his volunteers to make more ethical and environmental choices as they continued on with their lives after the experiment had finished.[7] It's a kind of version of the Overview Effect, but here on earth.

But as we've already touched on, this hardly suits our modern mentality. Look around and you'll find a self-driven, a distracted, and a fast-paced world. Stopping gets us nowhere, we're told. And so even when we do feel awe (even just the *tiniest* hint of it), the difficulty often comes with actually staying with it. It's inbuilt in us, societally, to make public immediately what we are experiencing, to 'have done it', then jump up and away for whatever comes next (because there is, always and inevitably, something next). How do we stay with wonder when we're so used to *doing*, to packing up our experiences and marking them as complete?

Fortunately, this *is* achievable. But it's important to work at it. Emotions have muscle memory. And so by allowing ourselves the time for awe – and when we do, by really forcing ourselves to stick with it – it's possible to habitualise it, to tap into it in a greater capacity in our daily lives.[8]

Because awe is the stop.

It doesn't have to be intimidating. A confidante of religion, awe is woven into the architecture of so many churches (elderly priests feed it daily on frankincense and other people's guilt). But it can also be found on a smaller scale. Those quiet spaces; those empty, ordered and whispered rooms of a museum or gallery – they can't help but make a home for numinous experience. Gallery as church (or the other way around, which so many of them now are). Keltner tells us that if we put a little effort in, we can feel awe every day. That it's all in the noticing. And it can be found just about anywhere, so long as we look hard enough. Once we stop taking the everyday for granted, we might notice awe-inspiring things everywhere we turn our heads. You don't need vast transcendence to be rendered awestruck – don't need your entire life suddenly sent spiralling out on a brand new trajectory. It could be drops of rain on a feather, making somebody laugh, the way the light falls – just for a moment. I watch videos of orcas and barnacled humpbacks that rise up, make their huge selves known out of the depths of my phone screen and disappear just as silent. I think of these creatures down there inside the ocean as I write this, and will again as you read it. I think of it all. How it is all there and happening right at this moment. Nothing is more real than now. What a thing! Remember it.

The planet and everything on it – all of it awesome. But we can't be in awe all the time, surely? We'd hardly get off the floor in all our wonderment.

IX

Still and Not So

THERE MUST BE A MIDDLE GROUND. The extravagant moments that have knocked me sideways those few times; those short, sharp, shocks into being that come blazing and rare (those somewhat secular mystical experiences): I cannot stand to live just this and nothing. Nor, though, would I give up the few moments of awe I've already experienced for anything less than the world. But let's, for the moment at least, leave them exceptional.

Another way, then, another option, is needed here for you and me both. An option where the real is to be found in the day-to-day, mixed up in those twenty-four hours of ours, so clear and pure we barely notice it.

Reality like water, of course.

And this reality, this wake up with me and slip me on and carry me lightly reality: *this* reality (just the same as awe, in fact), is also to be found in the noticing. Because it's only once you get really looking that you'll find it all and sundry. But hush now will you? Hush down and listen. See, though real can be the spark and *whomph* of a boiler flame or the tinny crack of a pull tab, it can be found in silence, too.

'I just need some quiet,' said Giorgio Morandi. And many times, at that, if we take the frequency of this particular phrase turning up in his letters as anything to go by.[1] Quiet is the theme that spills over his work – a whole life's worth of contemplative still lifes and simple, unpopulated landscapes. This output, and the hushed routine with which he lived his life, led him to be nicknamed *Il Monaco*, The Monk.

Morandi lived in Bologna, in a small apartment he shared with his three sisters and a thick layer of dust. 'It was a dense grey, velvety dust,' wrote the art historian John Rewald on visiting the studio, 'like a soft coat of felt, its colour and texture seemingly providing the unifying element for those tall boxes and deep bowls, old pitchers and coffee pots, quaint vases and tin boxes.'[2] The dust was all over the room and everything in it, and many of the artist's works have the appearance of having been painted in pastel tones before being dipped in a thick layer of the stuff. This same palette could be seen out of his studio window – it is a palette of earth and honeyed light, of dust that floats like clouds of small flies when the sun cuts through.

The line between art and reality is fine in Morandi's work. Each of his subjects – those white ceramic vases with their upward twist, tall glass bottles designed to hold one flower only, and squat little vases that have never even *heard* the word elegant – these were all often painted matte to emphasise their sturdiness and physicality. This has the effect of his objects holding the same reality on either of the planes you'll see them on – each existing with as much physicality on the canvas as in the studio. And in any of his paintings you feel you could reach in and pick one of the vases up right out of it, just as you'd have been able to off the shelves that lined the walls of his studio. Makes you wonder whether the whole point of it all was to work out how perfectly to depict three-dimensional space on flat canvas. Or whether he was only in it for that particular quality of Italian light; all those cluttered ceramics just a means to an end. Although cluttered is the wrong word – each composition could take weeks to set up.

'To achieve understanding,' Morandi once said, 'it is necessary not to see many things, but to look hard at what you do see.'[3] As ever, it's all in the noticing. And what if we took a leaf out of their book, these whispered compositions. What would happen if we just stepped right out of the rush and really stilled ourselves, what might we notice then? What if we turned away from it all, and decided to rest instead?

Rest is crucial in our search for reality. As we already know, we exist in a multiplicity of contradictions, and rest is one of them. We exist in today's world in a space that is anti-daydream but pro-reflection (because reflection implies improving for next time); a space that is against sleeping during non-traditional hours, but in favour of power naps – as long as they enhance achievement just as soon as we've woken up. Today is a space that is pro-rest but only on holiday – because this is rest that's been paid for, and rest so far out of our normal lives that we have to get on a plane to even get anywhere close to it. Even staying still has been capitalised.

I'm well indoctrinated into grind culture: this societal standard of ours that says that to succeed, we must be exerting one hundred percent of our effort at all times. This is why, even when I was bobbing about in the dark at Bristol Float Centre, I felt a strange guilt at not being able to see what the time was. It was this feeling that I was doing something slightly risky, as if time might falter and break without my constant tracking of it (in the small changing room where I've left my clothes, tiny Roman numerals drift off my watch face, and the twenty-four-hour clock slips to the bottom of my phone, where it falls to pieces). And it is also why, when people tell me my job sounds like a pretty sweet deal to them, I feel inclined to say, 'Actually, I am very stressed all the time', even though it is true that while writing this book I have done all kinds of strange and lovely things that would never make up anyone else's job description. We exist within the feeling that if we are enjoying, we are not working. Or that we have somehow beaten the system. But the system only exists because we are constantly feeding it.

And this thought is what has led me to where I am on this Saturday, curled up on yet another floor. I'm not entirely sure whether I've been asleep in this city-centre meeting room, but when I open my eyes I am aware of having come in from somewhere else. And also that there is a foot very close to my face.

The foot belongs to one of about twenty people scattered among the colourful cushions, rugs and blankets that fill the room. We are all here for the same reason: to participate in an afternoon of collective rest; an event inspired by the American poet, performance artist and activist, Tricia Hersey.

Maybe because rest is never a priority, my friend and I had arrived late and we'd found the door locked. As we stood cold and waiting in the square outside, we were aware that just a few metres away from us, rest was happening, as unattainable as it ever was. But the doorbell cut through the whispered space and we slipped into the room, eking a place for two on the warm wooden floor. And here we stretch, yawn and daydream; the room safe and soft as risen dough.

For Hersey, rest is a form of resistance: a radical, anti-racist, anti-capitalist and political act. 'Rest is a form of resistance,' she tells us, 'because it disrupts and pushes back against capitalism and white supremacy.'[4] And there *is* something, as one of the participants says afterwards, 'really fucking punk' about what we'd just done. See, capitalism is anti-rest. If we all rested, and, more to the point, *slept*, as much as we needed, we'd have an economic disaster on our hands.[5] With less sleep, you see, we consume more: more food; more coffee, certainly; and more advertising, with those tired and distracted eyes of ours. More advertising means of course more money (more to the corporations, that is, and less to us). But by resting, we turn away from this capitalist structure, we drop out of the race (limp back to the startline and beyond, to bed). 'Rest,' says Hersey, 'brings us back to our humanness.'[6] Rest brings us back to ourselves. Here, we refuse progress, cocoon ourselves into an absorbing and insular stillness either alone or tacitly shared. It is existence in a space that asks nothing more of us than to be. A space in which to slow, to breathe.

And with the breath in mind, I decide to take my search in another direction.

Which is exactly why, one Sunday afternoon, I find myself dripping wet in a circle of strangers dancing to Viking folk. This isn't what I want to talk about, though. See, when a day can feel like a dream, surreal moments like these become increasingly irrelevant.

My Wim Hof session falls on one of those tentative July days where you can't quite trust the warmth, and so everyone you see is dressed a little bit wrong. It also falls on a day that I am, for no discernible reason, feeling so dissociated I could get the same experience out of the next few hours if I was back at my flat just imagining how things might pan out. But instead I am in a small studio opposite a Safestore storage warehouse, lying on a yoga mat under dimmed lights. In front of me are two blue plastic tubs filled with one-degree water and sixty kilos of ice each. Of anyone, surely the Dutch extreme endurance athlete will be the one to manhandle me back into my body. His breathing technique, I've been told, will rebalance my parasympathetic and sympathetic nervous systems, bringing them back to their natural state, rather than one of chronic low-level stress. 'Breathe motherfucker,' Wim tells me. 'OK,' I reply. Because, as I've learnt recently, I do quite enjoy being told what to do.

The afternoon builds slowly towards our full-body immersion into the ice baths. But I want you only in this moment. Right where I am being told to breathe, again and again. Because in the same way as we can breathe our way *out* of stress, perhaps, I wonder, might we be able to breathe our way *into* a greater reality?[7] And it is right within one of these inhales that it comes calling once again. Oxygen touches me all the way down. I hold it. Find myself right there in the present. And this present is spacious and quiet. Never been so much emptiness behind my eyes; carries on and on. And here in the present, without past and future as a concern, it's an expanse that feels immeasurable. Pins and needles stripe down the entirety of my body until I feel I am made only out of horizontal lines, with each vibrating and setting the next off, and the next. Separate, but at the same time entirely together.

Walking home later, I feel more comfortable, more actually inside of my own body, than I have for a long time. I think of the American sergeant who told me to hold my breath when I found myself losing concentration. And how back then I immediately shunned her method, without realising that staying inside the breath would be where I was most likely to find reality.

People have long been aware of the spiritual connection between breath and the body. To sing one line of the Buddhist chant, *Oṃ maṇi padme hūṃ*, lasts six seconds, with a six-second inhale before the chant is repeated. In Kundalini yoga, *Sa ta na ma* again takes six seconds to sing, with the same six-second inhale in-between each line. And the *Om* chant, the sacred sound believed to resound through the entirety of the universe (the entirety of Bristol, certainly) should resound for six seconds exactly, with a pause of six seconds to inhale before its repeat. This same six-second breathing pattern can be found in prayer techniques the world over – in Japanese, African, Hawaiian, Native American, Buddhist, Taoist and Christian spirituality.[8] That six-second breath, it must be good for you. And give or take half a second, it certainly is. Biologically, the most efficient breathing rhythm for peak health is five-and-a-half breaths per minute (that's a five-and-a-half-second inhale with an exhale of the same length).[9] Our optimum lung capacity is a mirror to this, standing at five-and-a-half litres. As the perfect physical breath, it's no wonder that it has found its way into so many of our religions. And it's also no wonder, given it's so good for us, that the pattern gives believers a sense of physical wellbeing, thus increasing their responsiveness to the religious message.[10] We are calm and wide awake, but giving thanks in completely the wrong direction. It's not the divine, it's the breath that connects us all.

The day after my afternoon of collective rest I am scrolling down and across Instagram's never-ending double axis. I am hyper-aware to the sheer quantity of information thrown into my eyes, and so quickly too. It clangs about in my head, loud and shiny. Rest with technology is no rest at all, especially in our world when something so simple as a ping from someone else's phone or the noise of the same alarm that gets you up in the morning can have you spiralling into a stress state. Even *while* asleep, our blood pressure spikes in response to any noise just louder than the purring of a cat.[11] There it is once again. Stress. In its myriad forms, stress is at the absolute crux of dissociation, and any means through which we can diminish it (chipping away at its hard and plastic sheen) will only help us in our journey to live within a greater reality.

We're not the only ones stressed out by noise pollution. Existing in a world that is only getting louder is having negative effects on every species that makes use of sound to navigate, find food, attract mates and to avoid predators. And human-made noise is having a devastating effect inside our oceans, too. Any creature that uses echolocation as its form of communication and food sourcing may find themself both deaf and silenced, as great tankers lumber and groan across the surface of the water, and naval sonar devices send pulsating sounds into the depths at ever-increasing frequency.

There is a tiny limestone building, sitting stubborn on a Welsh cliff face, that can be found just above this noisy ocean of ours. When stormy, waves have been known to hurl themselves at its thirteenth-century face. But still the building stands. This is Saint Govan's Chapel. Looking from a ship, perhaps (somewhere out at sea, at least), you'd be lucky to spot it, it's that camouflaged within the rock. And from land, it's only when you come right to the cliff edge that you might notice steep and slippery steps. Head down them (carefully) and you will find yourself in a small single room. It's the simplest of interiors. A bare stone altar stands much older than the building's thick limestone walls – the saint is said to be buried below this, though nobody has been rude enough to unsettle him. Low benches line the interior and there is a basin for the priest to wash his hands in. The windows cast rectangles of white light on the opposing walls.

Saint Govan lived his life here as a hermit in the sixth century. He'd come over from Ireland and, stories say, landed here after being attacked by pirates off the Welsh coast. Desperate for a means of escape, he saw a fissure open right up in the rock: a miracle meant for one. And after his pursuers (mystified at his escape) had sailed off, Govan vowed to remain in the cave as a thanks to God and the cliff that had saved him.

Though the chapel we are standing in now was built over seven hundred years after the life of the saint, his miracle remains at its heart. One of the building's three doorways opens into the cave, with an altar built right next to it. You may be able to see grooves in the stone – said to be an imprint of Govan's ribs (as if he had wedged himself in, as close a fit to the rock as the chapel that would be built years from his death). He remained in this tiny elbow of land for the rest of his life, living on whatever he managed to grow in his wind-racked vegetable plot. What he harvested was small but always delicious (there's a beautiful simplicity that comes with eating a colour and just that).

Saint Govan wasn't alone in his solitude. His vocation – a full removal from society and concurrent devotion to solitude, penance and prayer – was popular among the early Christians; from the sixth century, the most pious of individuals were putting themselves purposely in the hands of nature at its least sympathetic.[12] (Many, in addition to their solitude, put their bodies through extreme trials, passing years atop single pillars, remaining standing always, or having themselves bricked up in inescapable cells. Others might go without shelter at all.) They were inspired by Old Testament saints like John the Baptist and Elijah before him, who made the journey of forty days and forty nights to Mount Horeb to hear the word of God: not in the usual Old Testament way (in claps of thunder, wind or earthquake), but in a 'still, small voice'.[13] The word hermit comes from the Greek 'eremos', meaning wilderness or an isolated place, and so 'eremites' literally means the inhabitants of such a landscape. And though many different landscapes were traversed in this shared effort, they were always the ones most associated with silence. They were deserts, mountains, islands and the poles.[14] Elijah certainly saw power in the quiet; it's no wonder he was such an inspiration.

Though it's not to say the hermits lived without sound completely. They lived with the waves that crashed to the shore, and the music of the rivers too. They lived with birdsong and the scuffling of animals in the unknown darkness. And they lived with the endless sounds of the weather. 'They chose to be alone with a God who was manifest in the wind,'[15] writes Alexandra Harris. And it is true, isn't it? There is nothing so minutely particular as a single gust of wind, or quite so generous as a breeze on a hot day. There never was something so accompanying when you happen to find yourself alone, either.

But it's not only in the silence. In the same way that silence can be the nudge we need to get back to ourselves, noise can work to exactly the same effect. See, while loud noise is bad for the health, loud music, on the other hand, is just its opposite.

Music was a part of the very earliest of civilisations. In 1995 a bone flute, made from the thigh bone of a young cave bear, was unearthed in the Divje Babe cave in west Slovenia, last picked up and played 60,000 years ago. And by a Neanderthal, too; probably never even touched by a human until its rediscovery. The bone fragment was found next to the remains of a fire pit[16] and there's something nice about knowing we've never got out of the habit of playing music beside the fire. (And maybe even then there was one who really just couldn't stand it; the same as when someone gets out a guitar around a campfire and you all have to listen, when all you wanted to do was to sit with the crackle of the flames and the bullshit conversations happening around you instead, and to continue having one of your own.) A good few years later, Homo sapiens were using bird bones to make instruments of their own.[17] Poor birds, made far too hollow. They have no choice, really, but to be associated, right down to their very insides, with song.

The music historian Suzanne G. Cusick defines it as a 'shared experience of being touched-without-being-touched by the vibrating air'.[18] In her translation, then, music is just another form of touch. And as we know, touch is so much nicer shared. When we sing together, we tap into something greater than ourselves. Communal singing, if we get down to the science of it, actually works to help us bond with each other – again, it's all in the connection. The activity releases oxytocin – remember, the bonding hormone – into our systems. Essentially, then, in a neurological context, our brains are telling us that singing together holds just the same intimacy as something like sex, or breastfeeding (both activities that release the hormone). And something else happens when we sing together. By holding the same notes and keeping to a shared rhythm, our breathing will begin to synchronise too. No longer existing as individuals, we become connected through our shared breath (we are the wash of a tide, we are more than ourselves). To sing together is to breathe together – and to breathe together means the synchronisation of our pulses, our hearts beat as one. Singing together, we become something larger than our own individual bodies, something more than our immediate selves.

And when it's loud enough, music taps into something more. Loud music is a stress reliever, flooding our bodies with endorphins and dopamine. It can be a multisensory experience, too: not just heard, but felt (low-frequency sounds make their presence known not only in our ears but right deep in our bodies). Loud music holds particular importance in my search because of its sheer power to overwhelm every other sense. It effectively takes over our brains, telling us to focus on one thing, and one thing only. There's that word focus again; keeps cropping up, doesn't it?

I don't think this has ever been made more evident to me than when watching Autechre, the Mancunian electronic duo so serious about focus that they play their sets entirely in the dark. And not half-hearted darkness, either. This is dark that takes itself seriously; darkness as physical an addition as a heavy curtain, rather than any pathetic lack of light. Though this is possibly enhanced because I am not only seeing them in a windowless basement, but a windowless basement in the middle of a long Glasgow winter. The room sweats and shudders, a jagged cave, a hot cocoon, a black box filled with fragments and fractals; it is an algebraic nightmare and impossible to dance to. 'I'm not a neuroscientist,' says Sean Booth, one half of the duo (you and me neither, Sean, but it doesn't seem to stop either of us going on about it), 'but all I know is that something happens in the dark. The music reaches further into you.'[19] This is an understatement. The music reaches and encroaches; enters right in and keeps on going. And with all visual stimulation out, I remember my mind focusing only on the sound. Because though silence can create a space within which to exist, it does so in exactly the same way that noise can. The thud and shake from the bass expel all thoughts. I am gripped hard and forced into the immediate; less a body and more there only as a single sense. More there as an existence that takes place solely within the sound itself – as if sound had one day just decided to change format, remodelling itself as a physical space. There I was, immersed *into* the real; the sound tied me to myself, to the darkness.

Back in Wales, the ocean-bitten grass is greener than anything you might ever have seen. It grows right out of the red clay soil – soil long believed to have healing properties (which as we well know, it always does, wherever you happen to find it). And it is right here, on the edge of this conversational sea, that I at long last begin to get a sense of my manifold themes all tying together. It's all here, right where I am. It's all here in the noise and the silence, the complete embodiment of this space; the land the sky the sea.

I'm close.

My dad and I standing small in a vast and frosted Mid-Wales landscape. There's no sides to it at all, just hills and onwards. Both of us are poorly dressed for the weather because we hadn't planned to be here; had been somewhere else entirely and happened to look up and notice just a few different groupings of them, starlings, all flying off in the same direction. So we thought to follow.

The sun sets just as we're looking at it. Sky over the snow-capped hills, all of it turning pink and giving the whole vista a raspberry and cream kind of texture. Later it was all ablaze in tangerine and it was then that hundreds of thousands of the things washed in over the woods and fields with a sound like ocean or fire (elemental, anyhow) as they landed immediate in the dark huddle of trees. And then up and away and again.

When we turn away, hurting with the cold, we leave them still swarming low over the woodland. And on and on and on.

Hundreds of thousands of the things. Typewritten on a dead white sky.

X

Composition

IT WAS THE TOGETHERNESS that I'll always remember from that afternoon murmuration. They're nothing with just a scattered few. It's like singing; for those starlings, it was all in the composition. And I think it might be all in the composition for us, too.

See, sometimes in life a moment is so beautifully composed, so made up of exactly the things you need, that reality takes its chance to sweep right on in as well.

One bright January afternoon I make my way across New York to the morose playground that fronts the Atlantic Ocean, Coney Island. The rides are still, boardwalk shops closed up for winter (wide streets only exaggerating the emptiness of the place). The only things open are a Starbucks and a Dunkin' Donuts, and I sit in one of them drinking something cold, tooth-achingly sweet and bright pink. Winter sun glints off the high metal fences that surround the fairground. On one I see a sign scrawled 'don't even *think* of parking here'. The day's so bright you might stub your toe on the shadows, they seem to be that solid. It's given the footprints in the sand a surreal depth to them. The clouds above me are wide and frittered.

I am here to join America's oldest winter swimming club, the Coney Island Polar Bears.

A few days before I do this I am sent a long waiver detailing all of the things that may or may not happen to me in and around the water. These range from getting quite cold to loss of consciousness and inevitably to death. And so I agree to blame myself for them all.

We get changed all together – somewhat fittingly – in the conference centre of the New York Aquarium. Here I meet a man who tells me he is the direct descendant of Shakespeare. And before I am introduced to his husband, I know that they had been in the same group therapy class for five years before they'd even started dating (which in hindsight I think should probably be the norm). The club president blows the whistle around his neck when he needs our attention, and on introducing me as an 'international guest' I get cheered.

We go down to the beach – all fifty of us, more maybe: one in a purple tinsel wig and a bow tie, another wearing a black and white Victorian striped bathing suit. I am barefoot and, because I'd not thought very far ahead in my plan, am wearing my swimming costume under quite a formal grey coat. There are thick gold chains and cowboy hats, and one man who looks like an overfed egg in red-orange rubber gloves the shape of lobster claws. The whole thing has a fiesta feel about it. I can't believe this happens every Sunday.

The water is burning and immediate.

And everyone whoops and cheers and screams and laughs. We jump up and down and under; every single one of us ecstatic and right there. None of us can stop smiling.

I float on my back and look across to the Ferris wheel and the rides, and then in the opposite direction to the distant skyscrapers far behind the wide and empty beach.

And there it was: a moment of perfect composition. An exquisite display of every component that makes up reality – sunlight (weather to push me into physicality), community (the proximity of other people to reassure me of my existence), touch (of the ocean, and the crowd around me), cold water and breath (which, at this temperature, took a full act of concentration). The pure physicality of it convinced me I could be nothing but real.

Afterwards there is a whole line of pink bodies leaning against the back wall of the aquarium warming up in the winter sun. They seem a part of the huge mural advertising the space. Or as if they are creatures more normally to be found inside, momentarily escaped from their tanks and languishing in their new-found freedom.

On the train back to the city I can't stop my teeth chattering, look out the window at the New York skyline and see it all there for the taking.

I return home to an English February.

My garden in the winter is a long stretch of moss and mud and leaves, and a tarmac path that decreases in size as the mulch of the grassless lawn spreads across it in the wet weather. It is shared with everyone in the building and everyone else's rubbish. All year round, grease-licked chicken boxes and small bits of plastic drift in under the gate. The garden is a useful depository for thieves. Late one night, a rowdy band of students clamber over the wall and demand to be let into the building. One of them has just had their phone nicked, and their Find My iPhone app has led them directly to my flat. They are adamant I am the culprit. It must have been chucked there by someone, I say, over the wall and into the ivy. They don't believe me and so, half asleep, I do the very unneighbourly thing of sending them to my neighbours, and go back to bed. One morning, two pet collars appear on the garden path. Each has been cut open with scissors, pet extracted.

The soil in my garden is cloddish and thick with the tangled roots of the tree that leans across the low brick wall dividing my garden from next door's. Next door employs a leaf blower, who gathers all of its leaves up neatly and takes them away with him. One day as I am carrying my bike out of the hall a huge and frantic black dog leaps over the neighbour's wall on the other side and takes a shit on my only surviving plant. I never see it again (neither the plant nor the dog). There is a cat that visits and pretends we are old friends only when my landlady happens to be visiting. It paws at my front door as if we have lived together for years, and my exclamations that I have never seen it in my life seem increasingly farcical – especially as I have asked more than once if I am allowed a pet. There is a blackbird, a giant and obnoxious pigeon, and the occasional squirrel.

Reality, see, it's in the noticing. Yes, it floods in with the perfect composition – something that can be found both in life and painting. But open our senses to it and we might discover it too as much in silence as in the thudding darkness. It is in the eye contact and the touch of others, the physical contact the outside world provides us too. If this really *is* true – if reality really *is* all in the noticing – then surely it means I can find it anywhere. That whether or not I can *feel* it at that moment, reality is just there; often out of reach, admittedly, but there and waiting. And just as it has appeared to me over so many years and in such sporadic waves, I can only hope there will come a day where it will make its dazzling self known to me, and that this time it will not leave.

As I write this the bulbs are waking up, pushing dark green from the soil that before looked only suffocating. There is, to count, exactly one snowdrop. It stands small and optimistic and in the way of a haughty clump of narcissi.

In truth, reality remains a slippery thing.

A NOTE ON THE FUTURE

In a future in which technology is bound to have an ever-growing presence in and on our lives, finding our sense of reality today is more important than ever.

And as this future advances towards us at a rollocking pace, please – for all our sakes – grasp hold of reality when you find it. Bind it to you and bring it forwards, however tangled and complicated this future of ours may turn out to be. And then you will only have to look inside your pocket, or down the side of your shoe; or perhaps you will have used it to tie up your hair – that scrap of reality you managed to hide and bring with you. And maybe it will have grown, and maybe it will be big enough to share. And maybe, just maybe, after all, we will find ourselves in a future in which we all feel real.

You do not need to leave your room. Remain sitting at the table and listen. Do not even listen, simply wait. Do not even wait, be quite still and solitary. The world will freely offer itself to you to be unmasked. It has no choice. It will roll in ecstasy at your feet.

FRANZ KAFKA

NOTES

1 Laing, Olivia, *The Lonely City: Adventures in the Art of Being Alone* (Edinburgh: Canongate Books, 2017, first published 2016), p. 22.

2 Thoreau, Henry David, *Walking* (New York: Dover Publications, 2019, first published as an essay in June 1862 in *The Atlantic Monthly*), p. 72.

1. PAINTING

1 Berger, John, *And Our Faces, My Heart, Brief as Photos* (London: Bloomsbury, 2005, first published 1984), pp. 72–3.

2 Letter from Vincent van Gogh to Émile Bernard, 1889, in Chipp, Herschel B., Theories *of Modern Art: A Source Book by Artists and Critics* (California: University of California Press, 1968), p. 44.

3 Berger, *And Our Faces*, p. 73.

4 'How The Brain Is Affected By Art' [article], *ACRM*, https://acrm.org/rehabilitation-medicine/how-the-brain-is-affected-by-art/. Accessed 11 January 2023.

5 'New Study Shows That Looking At Art Gives Same Pleasure As Being In Love' [video], *HuffPost* (18 May 2011, updated 6 December 2017), https://www.huffpost.com/entry/falling-in-love-with-art_n_861812. Accessed 2 February 2023.

2. MELANCHOLIA

1 Dixon, Laurinda S., *The Dark Side of Genius: The Melancholic Persona in Art, CA. 1500–1700* (Pennsylvania: Penn State University Press, 2013), p. 2.

2 Dixon, *The Dark Side of Genius*, p. 12.

3 Owens, Susan, *Spirit of Place: Artists, Writers & the British Landscape* (London: Thames & Hudson, 2020), p. 54.

4 Amiel, Henri-Frédéric, *Amiel's Journal*, Mary Augusta Ward (trans. 1885), https://www.gutenberg.org/files/8545/8545-h/8545-h.htm.

5 Dissociation is the umbrella term for depersonalisation (feeling unreal yourself) and derealisation (feeling the world is unreal).

6 'A Brief Guide to Working with Dissociative Identity Disorder', *Patient* (last edited 20 March 2014), https://patient.info/doctor/a-brief-guide-to-working-with-dissociative-identity-disorder#:~:text=DID%20is%20a%20well%2D researched,cent%20of%20the%20general%20population.&text=This%20 corresponds%20to%20between%20approximately,million%20people%20in%20 the%20UK. Accessed 23 July 2022.

7 Perkins, Joe, *Life on Autopilot: A Guide to Living with Depersonalization Disorder* (London: Hachette, 2021), p. 50.

8 Kenrick, Douglas T., 'Subselves and the Modular Mind' [article], *Edge*, https://www.edge.org/response-detail/10270. Accessed 21 July 2020.

9 Spaeth, Drake (Dr), 'Being Human in the 21st Century' [article], *Saybrook University*, https://www.saybrook.edu/unbound/being-human-in-modern-times/. Accessed 21 July 2020.

10 Davidson, Richard J. & Goleman, Daniel, *Altered Traits: Science Reveals How Meditation Changes Your Mind, Brain, and Body* (New York: Avery, 2017), p. 81.

11 Hari, Johann, *Stolen Focus: Why You Can't Pay Attention* (London: Bloomsbury, 2023, first published 2022), p. 173.

12 Nestor, James, *Breath: The New Science of a Lost Art* (London: Penguin Random House, 2021, first published by Riverhead Books, 2020), p. 149.

13 Baxter, Mark G. & Croxson, Paula L., 'Facing the role of the amygdala in emotional information processing' [article], *PNAS* (14 December 2012), https://doi.org/10.1073/pnas.1219167110. Accessed 5 March 2023.

14 Marchant, Jo, *Cure: A Journey into the Science of Mind Over Body* (Edinburgh: Canongate Books, 2016), p. 170.

15 Hoare, Philip, *Albert and the Whale* (London: 4th Estate, 2021), p. 117.

16 For full research on effects, see: Daws, R.E., Timmermann, C., Giribaldi, B. *et al.* (11 April 2022) 'Increased global integration in the brain after psilocybin therapy for depression', *Nature Medicine* 28, pp. 844–851.

17 Martinez, Rebecca, 'Dissociation as Medicine? Exploring Dissociation & Dissociative Psychedelics like Ketamine' [article], *Psychedelics Today*, https://psychedelicstoday.com/2021/07/12/dissociation-dissociative-drugs-ketamine-explainer/. Accessed 21 January 2023.

18 Young, Shinzen, 'The Dark Night' [blog post], *Shinzen's Blog* (13 November 2011), https://shinzenyoung.blogspot.com/2011_11_01_archive.html. Accessed 21 January 2023.

19 Laing, Olivia, *Funny Weather: Art in an Emergency* (London: Picador, 2020), p. 217.

20 Research carried out at the University of Chicago, cited in Laing, *Funny Weather*, p. 217.

21 Laing, *Funny Weather*, p. 217.

22 Laing, *Lonely City*, p. 43.

23 Kimmerer, Robin Wall, *Braiding Sweetgrass: Indigenous Wisdom, Scientific Knowledge and the Teachings of Plants* (London: Penguin, 2020, first published by Milkweed Editions, 2013), pp. 208–9.

24 Naftulin, Julia, 'Here's how many times we touch our phones every day' [article], *Insider* (13 July 2016), https://www.businessinsider.com/dscout-research-people-touch-cell-phones-2617-times-a-day-2016-7?r=US&IR=T. Accessed 6 February 2023.

3. SELF

1 Gisborne, Maria & Williams, Edward E., *Shelley's Friends: Their Journals and Letters* (Norman: University of Oklahoma Press, 1951), pp. 108–9.

2 Westerhoff, Jan, *Reality: A Very Short Introduction* (London: Oxford University Press, 2011), p. 59.

3 Goff, Philip, *Galileo's Error: Foundations for a New Science of Consciousness* (London: Penguin Random House, 2019), p. 149.

4 Bootle, Emily, *This Is Not Who I Am: Our Authenticity Obsession* (London: Ortac Press, 2022), pp. 2–3.

5 Hari, *Stolen Focus*, p. 117.

6 Nanay, Bence, '"Know thyself" is not just silly advice: it's actively dangerous' [article], *aeon*, https://aeon.co/ideas/know-thyself-is-not-just-silly-advice-its-actively-dangerous. Accessed 11 January 2023.

7 Moore, Thomas Gale, *On Progress* [ebook], p. 1, https://web.stanford.edu/~moore/Chapter1.pdf. Accessed 11 January 2023.

8 Isaiah 34:4.

9 Marchant, *Cure*, p. 219.

10 Kenrick, 'Subselves and the Modular Mind'.

11 Laing, *Funny Weather*, p. 218.

12 Sontag, Susan, *On Photography* (London: Penguin Random House, 2019, first published by Farrar, Straus and Giroux, 1977), p. 91.

13 Nanay, '"Know thyself" is not just silly advice: it's actively dangerous'.

14 Sontag, *On Photography*, p. 60.

15 Benderev, Chris, Nesterak, Max, Penman, Maggie *et al.*, 'Me, Me, Me: The Rise Of Narcissism In The Age Of The Selfie' [article], *NPR* (12 July 2016), https://www.npr.org/2016/07/12/485087469/me-me-me-the-rise-of-narcissism-in-the-age-of-the-selfie. Accessed 17 January 2023.

16 Haworth, Susan, 'Our ME, ME, ME Culture' [article], Cambios Coaching (26 October 2020), https://www.cambioscoaching.com/blog-posts-blog/2020/3/31/blog-with-newsletter-c2zwl-g54f9. Accessed 21 January 2023.

17 Benderev *et al.*, 'Me, Me, Me: The Rise Of Narcissism In The Age Of The Selfie'.

4. TOUCH

1 Marchant, *Cure*, p. 128.

2 Article in a mid-1990s edition of the magazine *Extropy: The Journal of Humanist Thought*. Cited in O'Connell, Mark, *To Be a Machine: Adventures Among Cyborgs, Utopians, Hackers, and the Futurists Solving the Modest Problem of Death* (London: Granta Books, 2018, first published 2017), p. 50.

3 Jensen, Eric, *Arts with the Brain in Mind* (Alexandria, US: ASCD, 2001), pp. 55–6.

4 Paul Klee quoted in Jaffé, Aniela, 'Symbolism and the Visual Arts' in Jung, Carl G. & von Franz, M. L. (eds.), *Man and his Symbols* (London: Dell Publishing, 1964), p. 292.

5 Ling, Eleanor, Munro, Jane & Reynolds, Suzanne, *The Human Touch: Making Art, Leaving Traces* (London: Paul Holberton Publishing, 2020), p. 15.

6 Crawford, Matthew, *The World Beyond Your Head: How to Flourish in an Age of Distraction* (London: Penguin Random House, 2015), p. 256.

7 Joyal, Christian C., Labrecque, Frédérike, Larouche, Émilie, Potz, Audrey (2021), 'What Is So Appealing About Being Spanked, Flogged, Dominated, or Restrained? Answers from Practitioners of Sexual Masochism/Submission', *The Journal of Sex Research* 58:4, p. 412.

8 Morin, Roc, 'That Time I Tried BDSM Therapy' [article], *The Atlantic* (26 October 2015), https://www.theatlantic.com/health/archive/2015/10/when-bdsm-is-therapeutic/412249/. Accessed 16 May 2022.

9 Joyal *et al.*, 'What Is So Appealing About Being Spanked', p.409.

10 Brennan, Cathy O., Edmondson, Amanda, J. & House, Allan O. (2016), 'Non-suicidal reasons for self-harm: A systematic review of self-reported accounts', *Journal of Affective Disorders* 191, p. 112.

11 Dixon, *The Dark Side of Genius*, pp. 14–18.

12 Dixon, *The Dark Side of Genius*, p. 90.

13 Goman, Carol Kinsey, 'The Art and Science of Mirroring' [article], *Forbes* (31 May 2011), https://www.forbes.com/sites/carolkinseygoman/2011/05/31/the-art-and-science-of-mirroring/?sh=77577efd1318. Accessed 7 September 2022.

14 Zanbon, Kat, 'How Engaging With Art Affects the Human Brain' [article], *AAAS* (13 November 2013), https://www.aaas.org/news/how-engaging-art-affects-human-brain. Accessed 15 June 2022.

15 Ling *et al.*, *The Human Touch*, p. 15.

16 Newberg, Andrew, cited in Marchant, *Cure*, p. 266.

17 Ling *et al.*, *The Human Touch*, p. 13.

18 Ling *et al.*, *The Human Touch*, p. 87.

19 Ling *et al.*, *The Human Touch*, p. 21.

20 John 20:25.

21 Goman, 'The Art and Science of Mirroring'.

22 Davies, William, 'How Feelings Took Over the World' [article], *The Guardian* (8 September 2018), https://www.theguardian.com/books/2018/sep/08/high-anxiety-how-feelings-took-over-the-world. Accessed 16 June 2022.

23 Nietzsche, Friedrich, *The Gay Science* (Cambridge: Cambridge University Press, 2008, first published 1882), p. 145.

5. LAND

1 Marchant, Jo, *The Human Cosmos: A Secret History of the Stars* (Edinburgh: Canongate, 2020), p. 21.

2 Letter from Paul Nash to Mercia Oakley, 1911, 'Paul Nash and the Wittenham Clumps: Early Works' https://www.nashclumps.org/early.html. Accessed 1 February 2021.

3 Fox, James, *Age of the Image* [documentary, episode 1], https://hdclump.com/age-of-the-image-episode-1/. Accessed 13 February 2023.

4 Owens, *Spirit of Place*, pp. 159–161.

5 Sontag, *On Photography*, p. 200.

6 Sontag, *On Photography*, p. 16.

7 Westerhoff, *Reality*, p. 58.

8 Nichols, *Blue Mind*, p. 80.

9 Westerhoff, *Reality*, pp. 96–7.

10 Thoreau, *Walking*, p. 10.

11 Thoreau, Henry David, *Walden* (London: Penguin Random House, 2016, first published 1854) p. 85.

12 Ansell, Neil, *Deep Country: Five Years in the Welsh Hills* (London: Penguin Books, 2012, first published by Hamish Hamilton, 2011), p. 45.

13 Thoreau, *Walking*, p. 66.

14 Laing, *Funny Weather*, p. 25.

15 Jones, *Losing Eden*, p. 24.

16 Hari, *Stolen Focus*, p. 199.

17 Wall Kimmerer, Robin, *Braiding Sweetgrass*, p. 236.

18 Thoreau, *Walking*, p. 2.

6. WATER

1 'What are Fractals?' [article], *Fractal Foundation*, https://fractalfoundation.org/resources/what-are-fractals/#:~:text=A%20fractal%20is%20a%20never,in%20an%20ongoing%20feedback%20loo. Accessed 7 February 2023.

2 Mandelbrot, Benoit, cited in 'How Mandelbrot's Fractals Changed the World' [article], *BBC* (18 October 2010), https://www.bbc.co.uk/news/magazine-11564766. Accessed 7 February 2023.

3 'Fractal Geography: Fractal Coastlines' [article], *Fractal Foundation*, https://fractalfoundation.org/OFC/OFC-9-4.html. Accessed 7 September 2020.

4 Nichols, Wallace, J., *Blue Mind: How Water Makes You Happier, More Connected & Better at What You Do* (London: Abacus, 2018), pp. 206–7.

5 Nichols, *Blue Mind*, p. 213.

6 Jones, *Losing Eden*, p. 95.

7 'Serotonin' [article], *Cleveland Clinic*, https://my.clevelandclinic.org/health/articles/22572-serotonin#:~:text=Serotonin%20plays%20several%20roles%20in,mania%20and%20other%20health%20conditions. Accessed 7 February 2023.

8 Jones, *Losing Eden*, p. 87.

9 Pearce, Kyle, 'Fractals in Nature: Develop Your Pattern Recognition Skills' [article], *DIYGenius* (4 November 2018), https://www.diygenius.com/fractals-in-nature/. Accessed 7 February 2023.

10 Guignon, Charles, *On Being Authentic* (New York: Routledge, 2005, first published 2004), p. 19.
11 Nichols, *Blue Mind*, p. 10.
12 Jones, *Losing Eden*, p. 88.
13 Marrin, D. L., 'The Waters of Chaos', *Magister Botanicus* (autumn 2007), p. 47.
14 Ovid, *Metamorphoses*, I.7–11. A.D. Melville (trans.) (Oxford: Oxford University Press, 1986).
15 Genesis 1:2.
16 Marrin, 'The Waters of Chaos', pp. 47–8.
17 Hoare, *Albert and the Whale*, p. 195.
18 Jeremiah 2:13; 17:13.
19 Dante, *Paradise*, 30.39. Dorothy L. Sayers & Barbara Reynolds (trans.) (London: Penguin Books, 1962).
20 Melville, Herman, *Moby Dick* (London: Oxford University Press, 1958), p. 1.
21 'What is the Evidence for a PRN' [article], *River Access For All*, http://www.riveraccessforall.co.uk/what_is_the_evidence.php. Accessed 7 February 2023.
22 Kenneth Clarke, *Leonardo da Vinci* (London: Folio Society, 2005), pp. 220–1.
23 Clarke, *Leonardo da Vinci*, pp. 220–2.
24 Lavin, Irving, 'Leonardo's Watery Chaos' [article], *Institute for Advanced Study* (2018), https://www.ias.edu/ideas/lavin-leonardo-chaos. Accessed 4 June 2023.
25 Lavin, 'Leonardo's Watery Chaos'.
26 Clarke, *Leonardo da Vinci*, p. 226.
27 Ovid, *Metamorphoses*, III.225–229.
28 Marrin, 'The Waters of Chaos', p. 48.
29 Eiseley, Loren, cited in Nichols, *Blue Mind*, p. 10.

7. SKY

1 Tokarczuk, Olga, *Drive Your Plow Over the Bones of the Dead.* Antonia Lloyd-Jones (trans. 2018) (London: Fitzcarraldo, 2022. First published 2009), p. 31.
2 Strand, Sophie, *The Flowering Wand: Rewilding the Sacred Masculine* (Rochester: Inner Traditions, 2020), p. 10.
3 Ehrenreich, Barbara, *Living with a Wild God: A Non-Believer's Search for the Truth About Everything* (London: Granta, 2014), p. 222.
4 Hoare, *Albert and the Whale*, p. 214.
5 Davidson & Goleman, *Altered Traits*, pp. 124–6.

6 Robert, Marie, *Keep it Together: Philosophy for Everyday Emergencies* (London: Scribe Publications, 2020, first published by Flammarion/Versilio, 2018), pp. 78–80.

7 Clottes, Jean, 'The Lascaux Cave Paintings' [article], Bradshaw Foundation, https://www.bradshawfoundation.com/lascaux/index.php. Accessed 21 May 2021.

8 Marchant, *The Human Cosmos*, p. 10.

9 Blanchfield, Theodora, 'The Psychology Behind Why We Care about Astrology' [article], *Verywell Mind* (14 July 2022), https://www.verywellmind.com/the-psychology-behind-why-we-care-about-astrology-5217929. Accessed 9 February 2023.

10 Beck, Julie, 'The New Age of Astrology' [article], *The Atlantic* (16 January 2018), https://www.theatlantic.com/health/archive/2018/01/the-new-age-of-astrology/550034/. Accessed 9 February 2023.

11 Prendergast, Clementine, 'Here's Why You've Become So Obsessed With Astrology' [article], *Vogue* (16 March 2021), https://www.vogue.co.uk/arts-and-lifestyle/article/obsesssed-with-astrology . Accessed 9 February 2023.

12 Neve, Christopher, *Unquiet Landscape: Places and Ideas in 20th-Century British Painting* (London: Thames & Hudson, 2020, first published by Faber & Faber, 1990), p. 130.

13 Marchant, *The Human Cosmos*, p. 115.

14 Marchant, *The Human Cosmos*, pp. 134–5.

15 Marchant, *The Human Cosmos*, p. 292.

16 Mondschein, Ken, *On Time: A History of Western Timekeeping* (Baltimore: John Hopkins University Press, 2020), p. 9.

17 Mondschein, *On Time*, p. 6.

18 Plato, *Timaeus*, 40b.

19 Kandinsky, Wassily, 'Reminisces / Three Pictures (1913)', in Lindsay, Kenneth & Virgo, Peter (eds.), *Kandinsky: Complete Writings on Art* (Boston: Da Capo Press, 1994), p. 361.

20 Harris, Alexandra, *Weatherland: Writers and Artists Under English Skies* (London: Thames & Hudson, 2016, first published 2015), p. 14.

21 Harris, *Weatherland*, p. 42.

8. HOMESICK

1 Cohut, Maria (Dr), 'Why Do We Need Nostalgia?' [article], *Medical News Today* (1 January 2021), https://www.medicalnewstoday.com/articles/why-do-we-need-nostalgia. Accessed 9 January 2023.

2 Jung, *Man and his Symbols*, p. ix.
3 Marchant, *Cure*, pp. 258–9.
4 Guignon, *On Being Authentic*, p. 31.
5 Prendergast, 'Here's Why You've Become So Obsessed With Astrology'.
6 Tempest, Kae, *On Connection* (London: Faber & Faber, 2020), 115.
7 Hayes, Nick, *The Book of Trespass: Crossing the Lines that Divide Us* (London: Bloomsbury, 2021, first published 2020), p. 229.

ABOUT AWE (A SMALL INTERLUDE)

1 'Awesome' [podcast], BBC Radio 4. https://www.bbc.co.uk/programmes/m001ghy5. Accessed 11 January 2023.
2 'Awesome' [podcast].
3 Marchant, *The Human Cosmos*, pp. 266–7.
4 'Awesome' [podcast].
5 Morgan, Eleanor, 'Oh wow! How getting more awe can improve your life – and even make you a nicer person' [article], *The Guardian* (23 September 2022), https://www.theguardian.com/lifeandstyle/2022/sep/23/how-getting-more-awe-can-improve-your-life-and-even-make-you-a-nicer-person. Accessed 9 January 2023.
6 Morgan, 'Oh wow! How getting more awe can improve your life'.
7 Marchant, *The Human Cosmos*, p. 267.
8 'Awesome' [podcast].

9. STILL AND NOT SO

1 Morandi, Giorgio cited in 'Giorgio Morandi' [article], *Tornabuoni Art*, https://www.tornabuoniart.com/en/viewing-room/giorgio-morandi-2/. Accessed 14 February 2023.
2 Rewald, John, in the Albert Loeb & Krugier Gallery exhibition catalogue for their May 1967 Morandi show (Taurus, 1967).
3 Morandi, Giorgio, cited in 'Giorgio Morandi' [article], *The Art Story*, https://www.theartstory.org/artist/morandi-giorgio/. Accessed 10 February 2023.
4 Hersey, Tricia, *Rest is Resistance* (London: Aster, 2022), p. 13.
5 Hari, *Stolen Focus*, p. 274.
6 Hersey, *Rest is Resistance*, p. 27.

7 Nestor, *Breath*, p. 41.

8 Nestor, *Breath*, p. 82.

9 Nestor, *Breath*, p. 104.

10 Nestor, *Breath*, p. 83.

11 Bosker, Bianca, 'Why Everything is Getting Louder' [article], *The Atlantic* (November 2019), https://www.theatlantic.com/magazine/archive/2019/11/the-end-of-silence/598366/. Accessed 10 February 2023.

12 Harris, *Weatherland*, p. 432.

13 1 Kings 19.

14 Maitland, Sara, *A Book of Silence* (London: Granta, 2008), p. 46.

15 Harris, *Weatherland*, p. 32.

16 'The Neanderthal Flute' [article], https://www.divje-babe.si/en/the-neanderthal-flute/#:~:text=The%20Neanderthal%20flute%20from%20Divje,the%20National%20Museum%20of%20Slovenia. Accessed 10 February 2023.

17 Owen, James, 'Bone Flute Is Oldest Instrument, Study Says' [article], *National Geographic* (24 June 2009), https://www.nationalgeographic.com/culture/article/bone-flute-is-oldest-instrument--study-says. Accessed 10 February 2023.

18 Cusick, Suzanne, G., 'Music as torture / Music as weapon', *Trans* 10 (2006), https://www.sibetrans.com/trans/articulo/152/music-as-torture-music-as-weapon. Accessed 10 February 2023.

19 Holbrook, Cameron, 'Autechre: "In the dark... the music reaches further into you."' [article], *mixmag* (16 July 2018), https://mixmag.net/read/autechre-in-the-dark-the-music-reaches-further-into-you-news/. Accessed 15 February 2023.

ACKNOWLEDGEMENTS

Thank you to my brilliant agent Holly Faulks. Your championing of *Pinch Me* from its inception has been invaluable. The same goes for my publisher Henry Rowley. I will be forever grateful for your unwavering support, for reading my synopsis and 'getting it' immediately.

Heaps of thanks to the many friends who critiqued early sections of the manuscript – in particular to Lotte Reford and Oriana Franceschi. And to all of you who have put up with my book being the main subject of every catchup we've had over the last three years.

To the unfoundedly generous Mike van Beinum and Kate Foster, for funding much of my reading material – thank you. And to Grace Attlee, for the perfect visualisation of the book's themes.

I am grateful to the Oppenheim Trust for the generous grant, and to both the Welsh National Writing Centre and The Arvon Foundation for lending me the physical (and head) space in which to write. I conducted my research in all kinds of unexpected places, and would like to extend my thanks to (nearly) all of those who allowed this to happen.

And thank you, of course, to my family, for your unfailing belief throughout.

IMAGE CREDITS

CHAPTER 1: PAINTING
Nature morte au pichet et aux pommes (1919) by Pablo Picasso

CHAPTER 2: MELANCHOLIA
Melencolia I (1514) by Albrecht Dürer

CHAPTER 3: SELF
Peinture (L'Etoile) (1927) by Joan Miró

CHAPTER 4: TOUCH
Pazzi Madonna (c.1425–1430) by Donatello

CHAPTER 5: LANDSCAPE
Landscape of the Vernal Equinox (1943) by Paul Nash

CHAPTER 6: WATER
A Deluge (c.1517–1518) Leonardo da Vinci

CHAPTER 7: SKY
Virgin Annunciate, from the exterior of the right panel of the Ghent Altarpiece (1432) by Jan van Eyck

CHAPTER 8: HOMESICK
The Expulsion from the Garden of Eden (c.1425) by Masaccio

CHAPTER 9: STILL AND NOT SO
Natura morta (1950) by Giorgio Morandi